Hot Mess: A Practical Guide to Getting Organized

Hot Mess: A Practical Guide to Getting Organized

Laurie Palau

N-13: 9780692921623
N-10: 0692921621
ry of Congress Control Number: 2017948974
zc.opublishing, New Hope, PA

For Josh, Zoe, & Logan who know what it's like to live with a Hot Mess.

Table of Contents

Introduction

FOR THOSE OF YOU I haven't met, I'd like to introduce myself: My name is Laurie Palau. I am a mother, wife, daughter, entrepreneur, speaker, coach, writer, and friend. I am not defined by any one of those roles individually, but collectively they shape every action that takes place in my life.

I am flawed, authentic, strong, decisive, and honest. In 2009, at the height of the recession, I started a professional organizing business called Simply B Organized. Many people thought I was nuts to embark on a new venture during such unsettling times, but in my crazy mind, I thought, "What better time to help people then during a crisis?"

I have an outspoken "tell it like it is" personality (as you will read in the coming pages). I believe in "tough love," accountability, and independence, but don't mistake that for not caring. I love to teach, inspire, motivate, and empower people. I believe in leading by example. I want people to know they are not alone. My clients know this, my friends know it, my family knows it, and now you know it.

Will you ever walk into my house and see a pile of papers? Of course you will. Will you ever see laundry that needs to be put away? Yep. So take that image of a "Martha Stewart," nothing-ever-out-of-place home and throw it out the window.

Good. Now let's get down to business….

When I sat down to write this book I didn't want it to be another "how to get organized" manual. We all know there are enough of them out there! I'm not going to tell you that you should become a minimalist or that you should fold your t-shirts a certain way.

As an organizing expert, I have read and researched countless books, blogs, and articles on how to be organized, and if there is one thing I have learned, it's that there is no "right way" to organize your life. The most successful methods are the ones that are simple and sustainable.

So how is my approach different? My philosophy begins with getting to the root of your clutter. Like any ailment, you can treat the symptom, but until you get to the root of the problem, it will continue to come back. Clutter is no exception. Once you can identify where your clutter is coming from, and why it's holding you back, you can begin to implement strategies to eliminate it once and for all.

My goal isn't to get you to throw everything away, but rather to teach you some strategies that allow you the freedom to remove unnecessary clutter from your life without guilt, fear, or anxiety.

Everyone has a unique story. Everyone has struggles (present company included), so whatever prompted you to read this book, congrats for taking the first step. Allow this book to be your roadmap and a reminder that you don't need to face your challenges alone.

The fact that you picked up this book in the first place shows that you want to make a change, so pat yourself on the back for recognizing that you could benefit from some guidance. Whether you borrowed this book from a friend or purchased it yourself, you're investing time in reading it, and for that I thank you.

My therapist once told me: "You don't need to be perfect, you just need to be good enough." You know how every now and again you hear a comment that resonates with you? Well, that one resonated with me. In seeking perfection, I was constantly trying to achieve something that didn't exist. Once I freed myself from that unattainable goal, I was able to set realistic expectations for both my family and me. I want the same for you.

If nothing else, here are three goals I hope you accomplish at the conclusion of this book:

1) **Feel Inspired:** Choose some new or improved strategies that inspire you to declutter at least one area of your life.

2) **Laugh:** I want you to be entertained. Life can be difficult. It can be stressful. It can be overwhelming. Finding humor in the chaos is a reminder that it's not all bad, and you are not alone.

3) **Pay It Forward:** Think of at least one person who can also benefit from some of these strategies and pay it forward by recommending this book.

So curl up with a glass of wine, a cup of tea, or another beverage of your choice, and let's toast to the beginning of a more organized life, because after all, aren't we all a bit of a hot mess?

"Clutter isn't limited to what you
see on the outside, it's about how it
makes you feel on the inside."

—LAURIE PALAU

Part I: Clutter

———

BEFORE YOU CAN BEGIN THE organizing process, it's important to understand the root of your clutter. Getting organized has more to do with changing your behavior than owning the right products. The first several chapters are dedicated to helping you recognize your clutter pitfalls and how to avoid them.

CHAPTER 1

What Is Your Clutter Costing You?

———

WHETHER WE REALIZE IT OR not, clutter effects us both emotionally and financially. See if you can relate to any of the following statements:

* I wish my home didn't look so cluttered.
* I am tired of feeling stressed as soon as I walk through the door.
* I waste time looking for stuff I know I have, but can't seem to find.

If you answered YES to any of the above statements, I can assure you of two things: First, you are not alone, and second, you are going to be so glad that you picked up this book.

There are lots of reasons how and why clutter infiltrates our lives, but the one thing we all have in common is the feeling of frustration when we look for things that we know are there, but can't seem to find. Whether it's your keys, your sunglasses, or your kids' cleats, misplaced items increase stress, produce anxiety, and can set a negative tone for the day. Yet so many of us continue to live in a permanent state of disarray.

Guess how much time the average American wastes each day looking for things? 55 minutes[1], that's almost one hour! That is a lot of time. Maybe it's 10 minutes here, 10 minutes there, another 15 minutes somewhere else, but it adds up. If you are anything like me, you don't have an extra five minutes to spare, let alone 55! Can you imagine what you would do with an extra hour in your day? Read, exercise, catch up with a friend, take a nap—the list is endless.

What's even more astonishing is how that hour of lost time accumulates to seven hours each week, and 30 hours each month. By the end of the year, the average person has wasted 365 hours as a result of disorganization—more than two weeks! That is longer than some people's annual vacations.

Many of you reading this may be nodding your head in agreement, but for many, it has gotten to a point of acceptance, or "it is what it is." In other words, "This is my crazy, chaotic life and there's nothing I can do about it."

But that's just not so.

I'm here to tell you your life doesn't have to be a cluttered, chaotic mess.

Now I'm going to ask you what I ask all of my clients: **"What is your clutter costing you?"**

---

1 Newsweek Staff (June 04, 2004). *Clean Freaks*: Newsweek. Online: http://www.newsweek.com/clean-freaks-129009

When I ask people that, I often get a quizzical look. People aren't sure how to answer me. They wonder how do I put a price tag on my disorganization? But I'm not solely talking about money; I am also referring to intangibles:

* Anxiety
* Frustration
* Sanity
* Time

Another word for *clutter* is *chaos*. So as you begin to remove clutter from your life, you reduce the amount of chaos that surrounds you. This book is a step-by-step guide for taking you from chaos to calm.

Once you reduce your clutter, you can reclaim time, increase your productivity and spend more time doing what you love. If you do this, you should see an increase in your self-esteem, patience, and appreciation of your home and the stuff in it.

CHAPTER 2

Defining Clutter

———

BEFORE WE GET TOO FAR, I think it's important that we all get on the same page. For most people, the word clutter conjures up scenes from Hoarders, or Grey Gardens with its mazes of magazines lining the hallways. You may even imagine feral cats, rodent droppings, and indistinguishable mounds of who-knows-what.

I'll be honest; I can count on one hand (with three fingers to spare) how many times I've encountered a true hoarder. Yup, twice—you guessed it! It was very early in my career as a professional organizer, and it didn't take me long to realize it wasn't the right fit for me. It's not so much that I was in over my head (no pun intended); the reality is that their struggles go deeper than piles of paper, overflowing loads of laundry, and rooms filled with toys. I am not a licensed psychologist, although I often like to think of myself as one, and the level of help they need is beyond what I can offer.

The majority of my clients are like you and me. Their days are spent running between work, school, PTA meetings, soccer practice, dance lessons, grocery shopping, overseeing homework, making dinner, looking after ailing parents, and whatever else we can fit into our days.

The result of all this life-madness is often a cluttered home, and with that, I can help. The first step is having the will to change, and the second step is actually doing it. The whole process can be overwhelming, but I am going to break it down step by step so even a kindergartener can get it.

Let's talk about what I like to call "the other C-word:" CLUTTER.

Most people have some level of clutter in their homes (including yours truly). Let's be honest—we don't live between the pages of a magazine, on a Pinterest board, or in an HGTV show. We are all real people with lives, hobbies, jobs, and families. And with all of that comes *stuff.*

Accept that there is going to be a certain level of clutter in your life. How much, though, is up to you.

Define your clutter; don't let your clutter define you.

Clutter means different things to different people. In its most basic form, clutter means **disorder.** To tackle your clutter issues, you need to identify what is causing your disorganization.

Yes, it's undeniable that physical clutter gets in our way, but understanding *how* and *why* clutter gets there in the first place is the first step in decluttering your life forever.

Instead of thinking about your clutter as a huge mountain of garbage, take a step back and ask yourself, *"What is the root cause of this mess?"* When I think about clutter, I like to break it down into three main groups: Physical, Emotional, and Calendar.

Integrated Clutter Model

We will get into specifics in later chapters, but for now I just want to get you thinking.

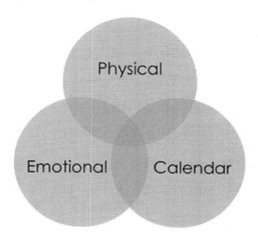

Below is a brief overview of each type:

1) **Physical Clutter:** Physical clutter is easy to define. It's the volume of stuff you have around you: Toys on the floor, papers on a desk, miscellaneous stuff in a garage, or extra furniture in a basement. You get the idea. People go through various stages in their lives and stuff naturally follows suit.

Think about overflowing closets, a filled garage or attic, a home office that makes you want to turn around and shut the door—that is what I call physical cutter.

2) **Emotional Clutter:** Emotional clutter is what holds us back from getting rid of something that we no longer need or use. Typically, it stems from two things: Guilt or fear.

"My Aunt Edna gave this to me, so I should keep it". = GUILT

"These shoes kill my feet and I'll never wear them again, but I spent a fortune on them." = GUILT

"What if I need that statement from the gas company and I don't have it?" = FEAR

"I can't get rid of those extra dishes; what if I suddenly need them?" = FEAR.

3) **Calendar Clutter:** Calendar clutter has to do with how you account for your time. Whenever you hear someone say, "I just don't have the time to get everything done," they are probably suffering from calendar clutter. In the spirit of full transparency, this is where I struggle most.

Example: *You work all day, then spend the hours from 4 to 8 PM running your kids between soccer practice and dance—and did someone mention making dinner? Then there's homework and showers. Before you know it, you're cross-eyed and cranky, and the only thing calling your name is a glass of wine or your bed!*

Okay, so I may have just shared with you what a typical Tuesday night looks like at my house, but even if you don't have kids (or kids living at home), calendar clutter can still get in your way.

Whether you are a workaholic who spends 80 hours a week at the office, a stay-at-home mom who spends all day running from activity to activity, or someone busy taking care of ailing parents, finding time to organize your house doesn't always seem doable.

The key to remember is emotional clutter and calendar clutter almost always result in physical clutter.

Most people typically have one dominant type of clutter, but they are all intertwined. In the coming chapters, we are going to take a closer look at each of these three types to help you identify the root cause of your clutter. Identifying your dominant source of clutter is the first step in your path to living more simply.

CHAPTER 3

Identifying Your Dominant Clutter Source

————

NOW THAT WE'VE TALKED ABOUT the different types of clutter, you should have a better idea of your dominant type. As I said, you probably have some overlap, since both emotional clutter and calendar clutter usually result in physical clutter. The key takeaway is to identify the root of your clutter so you can change the behavior that's holding you back.

It's important to understand not just your triggers, but your family's too. I know, for instance, that I don't have much emotional clutter, but my youngest daughter does. She struggles with forming attachments to things (poetic justice for someone like me, don't you think?). As a result, I need to tailor my approach with her differently than with my older daughter, whose room is usually a mess because taking time to organize things is not a priority for her. Does that make sense?

One of my favorite books is *The 5 Love Languages: The Secret to Love That Lasts* by Gary Chapman (Northfield, 2014). For those of you who are not familiar with the book, Chapman believes that there are five main communication styles that individuals use to show love in their relationships: Gifts, acts of service, words of affirmation, physical touch, and quality time. What I find so interesting about his philosophy is that we often assume that what resonates with one person can be used across the board for everyone. Not true! In order to effectively communicate with others, it's important to know not just your love language, but also theirs. The same principle holds true for clutter.

If you've ever argued with your spouse or kids about the importance of picking up after themselves, or helping out around the house, you know that to get them to do what you want, you often need to adjust your tactics. When I first read Chapman's book, it was like a light bulb went on in my head. It didn't take me long to realize that my older daughter's love language is acts of service, while the younger one's is time.

Once I recognized what motivates them, I was able to adjust my approach and get them to do what I asked. More importantly, I found that I spent a lot less time beating my head against the wall or screaming like a lunatic!

Let me elaborate: My older daughter's drive comes from helping others, so if I want her to do something, like put her laundry away, I say something like: "The sooner you put away the laundry, the more time you will have to go over to your friends to help her out." Since the value to my daughter is doing something for others, she is more inclined to do what I say without a fight.

With my younger daughter, whose love language is time, I might say, "The sooner you put away your laundry, the more time we will have to sit on the couch and watch TV." If I used that approach with my older girl, she would probably roll her eyes! But for my younger daughter, it's an incentive.

At the end of the day, I got them both to put away their laundry, but my approach was different based on what the value was to each of them. The same principle holds true for understanding the root of each person's clutter.

Once you understand the root of the clutter created by you and those around you, you can truly begin to make significant changes in your life. I've created this quiz to help you identify your dominant clutter source.

1) What was your childhood home like growing up?
   a. I lived in a house filled with clutter.
   b. My parents saved nothing (I have no physical childhood memorabilia).
   c. Everything had a place and my parents made sure to keep the house organized.

2) What is the leading reason for your clutter?
   a. I have too much stuff and not enough space.
   b. I am emotionally attached to things and find purging difficult.
   c. I just don't have enough time to get organized.

3) My attempts at getting organized seem to fail because:
   a. I don't have the right system for my belongings.

    b.   I quit midway through my project due to feeling overwhelmed.

    c.   I start multiple projects and never see anything through to completion.

4) What would you say is your biggest roadblock for getting organized?
    a.   Not knowing what to do with my stuff.
    b.   Having fear or guilt about getting rid of things.
    c.   Not having enough time to declutter and organize my things.

5) I do everything around the house otherwise it won't get done.
    a.   True
    b.   False

6) I have a hard time saying no when people ask me to do something.
    a.   True
    b.   False

7) Guilt stands in my way of decluttering.
    a.   True
    b.   False

8) If I had more time I would be organized.
    a.   True
    b.   False

9) We could open up a store with the amount of
_____ we own (fill in the blank with what you
tend to accumulate, such as sports equipment, shoes,
or books).
    a. True
    b. False

Scoring:

Questions 1-4: If you answered A to at least 3 questions,
you most likely struggle most with physical clutter. If you
answered B to at least 3 questions, emotional clutter is weigh-
ing you down. If you answered C to at least 3 questions, then
calendar clutter is your dominant source.

Question 5: If you answered true, add one to calendar
clutter.

Question 6: If you answered true, add one to calendar
clutter.

Question 7: If you answered true, add one to emotional
clutter.

Question 8: If you answered true, add one to calendar
clutter.

Question 9: If you answered true, add one to physical
clutter.

If your answers were more evenly split, you probably
wrestle with two types of clutter, but the one with the majority is more than likely your dominant source.

My dominant clutter type is _____.

We are going to dig a little deeper into each of the clutter types in the coming chapters so be sure to read on! I recommend reading about each of the different types, not just your own, since you may have to deal with someone who has a different dominant source than you; understanding their struggles will help you to better communicate with them.

CHAPTER 4

Physical Clutter

———

PHYSICAL CLUTTER IS EASY TO describe. It's an excess of STUFF: papers, toys, clothes, shoes, sports equipment, tools, and so on.

Physical clutter results from one of two things:

1) More stuff than space (which we call " a volume issue")

2) An improper system for organizing your things

VOLUME

You don't have to be a math wiz to realize that if you have more stuff than space, you're going to end up with clutter.

According to a Gallup poll[2], the average American family spent approximately $830 per child on Christmas presents in 2015, which was an increase of more than $100 from the prior year.

---

2 Saad, L. (Nov. 16, 2015). *Americans plan on spending a lot more this Christmas*. Princeton, NJ: Gallup. Online: http://www.gallup.com/poll/186620/americans-plan-spending-lot-christmas.aspx

There is so much "keeping up with the Joneses" that kids don't even know why they are asking for half the things they say they want. Many adults are no better. According to *Forbes* magazine[3], women now have over 30 outfits in their closets—that's one for every day of the month!

I'm not here to lecture you about how much you buy for yourself or your kids, but I will tell you that there is a direct correlation between excess material items and clutter. We live in a society of "bigger, better, more," and keeping up with the Joneses makes the mantra hard to resist. How many times have you purchased the hottest item for the holidays only to see it go unused two months later? How about those shoes you *had to have*, but realized weren't so great after all?

Before we can start to reduce the volume of stuff in our homes, we need to rethink *why* we bring it into our lives in the first place. Chances are that your kids gravitate to the same games and toys day after day, and that week after week, you're grabbing the one pair of jeans that makes you look and feel good, despite having a dozen others in the closet.

Pareto's Principle

Otherwise known as "the 80/20 rule," Pareto's principle[4] can be applied to most areas of physical clutter.

---

3 Johnson, E. (Jan. 15, 2015). *The real cost of your shopping habits.* Forbes. Online: https://www.forbes.com/forbes/welcome/?toURL=https://www.forbes.com/sites/emmajohnson/2015/01/15/the-real-cost-of-your-shopping-habits/&refURL=&referrer= - 76d0b0571452

4 For an overview of Pareto's principle, visit: https://en.wikipedia.org/wiki/Pareto_principle

- We wear 20% of our clothes 80% of the time.
- Kids play with 20% of their toys 80% of the time.
- We use 20% of the goods in our homes; the remaining 80% ends up untouched.

Okay, you get it. We have too much stuff. However, there are times when physical clutter results from not having the right storage or not knowing how to maximize your space.

MAXIMIZING YOUR SPACE

I've worked with many clients who live in small apartments or older homes with tiny closets, and despite frequent purging, they still can't seem to get organized. Often, it's a matter of building or buying the best system for your space and needs.

For example, one client—let's call her Susan—lives in an adorable home built in the 1920s. Despite her home's charm, it lacks modern amenities like a large pantry, tall cupboards, or pullout shelving. With two small kids, a husband, and a dog, she needed to come up with a system that allowed her to see what she had without hassle.

After assessing her habits and contents, we determined that Susan is a visual person—meaning she needs to see her items in order to be productive (I'll help you find your organizational style in a later chapter). We also determined that it would be most effective if she utilized clear containers so she could easily identify their contents at a glance. And we decided a modular stacking system would be best for her and her husband, since they are both tall, and these would allow her to maximize the vertical space of her small pantry. Finally, we chose to add some inexpensive rollout shelves for canned goods, which would allow her to access them easily, rather than blindly reaching to the back to find what she needs or having stuff get "lost."

In Susan's case, it wasn't a volume issue; it was simply a matter of not having the right systems for her needs. Two years later, her kitchen is still uncluttered and organized, proving that the right system can make a difference.

―――

Three Tips for Mastering Physical Clutter

1) **Scale your volume to match your space**. Most people have more stuff than space. This may require you to make some initial tough choices. If you want to maintain an organized space (whether it's a garage, pantry, or closet), you have to factor in the space you have available. Someone with a big walk-in closet can get away with keeping 40 pairs of shoes neat and organized, whereas someone with a tiny reach-in closet is either going to have to purge or get super creative with storage.

    Remember Pareto's Principle: Whether your downfall is clothes, shoes, tools, toys, or household items, we only use 20% of the items we own. Start by prioritizing those items. You're probably thinking to yourself, "easier said than done." You love all of them! How are you going to choose? Here are a few questions to help you navigate the process:

- Do I love it?
- When am I going to wear it again?
- When was the last time it got used/worn?
- Would I miss it if it were gone?
- How often do I use/wear it?

The great thing about these questions is that they are generic enough to be used in a variety of areas, from closets to toys. If your kids no longer play with something, donate it, pack it away for younger siblings, or relocate it to an attic, garage, or basement for memorabilia storage (which we cover in a later chapter).

You want your space to be able to breathe—meaning that you don't want it jam-packed so that each time you open the door you have to duck for cover in fear of something toppling on you! My next two rules for mastering clutter can help you maintain the volume you decide is right.

2) **Purge frequently**. I'm not suggesting you subscribe to the "one in, one out" rule, but if you know you are a shopper, be mindful of how often you bring new items in the home. Consider how often you cycle out the old. There's no hard and fast rule for how often this needs to happen. Different areas of the home will require more frequent maintenance. If

you have a particular area that keeps getting messy, start there.

For example, if your entryway or mudroom is a revolving door of jackets, shoes, and backpacks, you may need to spend 10 minutes each week sorting through things that don't need to live there. Sweatshirts and shoes have a way of making their way from the kids' bedrooms and setting up camp like protesters at a march. Weed out the unnecessary. Return some things to their rooms, and allow yourself to see what you have without having to dig through mounds of clutter. If you get into the habit of doing this routinely, I suspect you'll notice a decrease in stress and feel less overwhelmed.

I also strongly recommend getting family members on board to share the workload. If your kids are old enough, have them go through and organize their hats, gloves, hoodies, and jackets. If everyone pitches in, it goes a lot quicker. If you look at your patterns of behavior, you will probably realize that some spots require more TLC than others.

3) **Think before you buy.** We all like getting new things, but the next time you are shopping, ask yourself the following questions:

   * **Where am I going to put this?** How many times have you browsed the aisles of HomeGoods and brought home an amazing treasure, only to find

you have nowhere to put it? Just because you love something, doesn't mean it is going to look good in your house. If you have limited counters in your kitchen, think twice before buying another cookie jar, vase, or ceramic bowl.

* **When am I going to wear this?** The same rule of thumb holds true with clothing. Just because you see something adorable, doesn't mean you should buy it, especially if it's for a special occasion. Women notoriously have closets filled with dresses that they wore once to an event, but have no plan to ever wear again. Before you whip out the Nordstrom's credit card, consider borrowing something from a friend, or taking advantage of sites like Rent the Runway (renttherunway.com), which let you rent high-end, designer dresses for a fraction of their value; once you are done with them, you simply ship them back!

* **How often am I going to use this?** This is a great follow-up question to the first two. Maybe you have a spot for whatever impulse buy you make, but are you *really* going to use it, or do you just like it? I can think of plenty of things I see throughout the day that I like, but that doesn't mean I should buy them. Let me give you an example. I can't stand carrying purses. Half the time I go somewhere, I leave mine in the car and just take my phone and keys with me. Yet, I

love admiring purses: Tory Burch, Michael Kors, Ted Baker, to name a few. But just because I like them, doesn't mean I'm going to use them. Being able to make that distinction is a huge step in reducing physical clutter from your life.

In sum, be mindful of what you bring into your home before it enters the front door. The next time you are faced with whether or not to make an impulse purchase, pause and ask yourself these questions. If you don't have a solid answer, you know it's time to pass.

Side note: I am the buzzkill of all my friends. Whenever we go shopping, I always ask the aforementioned questions. I get more eye rolls and under-the-breath swearing than I care to admit! I'm not trying to be Debbie Downer. I just know that, once the novelty of the purchase wears off, they are going to be stuck trying to figure out what to do with it.

CHAPTER 5

Emotional Clutter

———

EMOTIONAL CLUTTER STEMS FROM HOW you feel. It's an emotional connection that makes you feel compelled to keep something. Unfortunately, the problem with this type of clutter is that it stems from sentiment, not logic, and as a result, you end up with a bunch of physical clutter.

Emotional clutter typically results from one of two things:

- **Guilt:** *"My kid made this so I can't throw it away."*
- **Fear:** *"What if I need it someday."*

GUILT

One of the most common roadblocks in the path to decluttering is GUILT. Guilt can weigh you down and paralyze you from moving forward.

Does either of these scenarios sound familiar to you?

"Aunt Jane gave me this vase for my wedding. Even though I don't like it, I feel badly getting rid of it. What if she comes over and asks to see it?"

"I spent a lot of money on these shoes and even though they kill my feet and I'll never wear them, I can't bear to get rid of them."

Guilt is by far one of the biggest hurdles to overcome when purging.

———

FEAR

The other major culprit of emotional clutter is FEAR, otherwise known as the "what if" factor. You see this a lot with paper clutter. For example, people tend to hold onto bank statements, bills, and user manuals, even though the majority can be accessed online.

Remember when I talked about the Pareto Principle in the last chapter? I mentioned we don't ever look at 80% of the paper we hold onto. We are accumulating clutter in our lives out of fear that we may need to reference it someday, when more than likely we won't. Let me ask you, how often have you had to go back and reference an old bill from Bloomingdales? I'm guessing probably never.

I guarantee that somewhere in your house is either a stack of papers to be filed or a full cabinet of outdated and unnecessary paperwork that you're holding onto "just in case."

It's understandable; we learned this behavior from past generations. Before the Internet or Google, if you needed a past bank statement, you'd have to call the bank and have them send it by snail mail. Similarly, if your washing machine broke, you would need the manual to troubleshoot the problem. Thankfully, today it's quicker and easier to look up what you need online, thus eliminating the need to hold onto these things. You heard me ... throw the manuals in the recycling bin!

True story: A couple of years ago my washing machine stopped working. A flashing error message came up on the front panel, so you know what I did? I took a picture with my phone, went to my computer, and Googled "E4" and the model number. Within seconds I was staring at a YouTube video and three articles on the cause and how to fix it. It would have taken me 10 times as long to find and page through the manual.

Rule of thumb: If you can access what you need online, chances are you don't need it in physical form. In other words, pitch the paper!

I asked my accountant, Peter Augenblick, of <u>Augenblick & Company Accountants and Auditors</u> in New Hope, Pa., to compile a quick cheat-sheet of how long the IRS requires you to keep certain documents. However, I encourage you to confirm with your accountant if you have specific questions.

Federal Income Tax Returns	Open for examination for three years from the later of the due date, including extension, or the date it was filed. *No expiration of examination of fraudulent tax returns.
State Tax Returns	Many states, including Pennsylvania where I live, have no statute of limitations.
Legal Agreements	Retain all paper while agreement is in force. Examples: Marriage certificates, loan documents, insurance policies, and wills.
Other Transactions (e.g., monthly statements)	Keep recurring transaction documents until the next transaction. Most statements are available online.
Things to Consider	If the vendor (e.g., accountant, attorney, bank) retains the paperwork, you should always have a paper trail. If in doubt, scan! Scan! Scan! And store in a folder on your computer.

Tips for Working Through Emotional Clutter:

If you're someone who struggles to part with things, try using the WHO, WHAT, WHERE, WHEN, WHY strategy:

1) **WHO gave it to you?**

Chances are, we can't remember where half the stuff we have came from. Unless the item has specific sentimental value, if you're not using it, consider donating or selling it.

2) **WHAT purpose is it serving?**
If something is just sitting on a shelf, taking up space, ask yourself if someone else could benefit from having it.

3) **WHERE am I keeping it?**
If the answer is: Shoved inside a closet, basement, garage, drawer, or anything similar, you should probably consider either moving it to memorabilia storage, donating it, or selling it (not to worry, we get to each of these options in a later chapter!).

4) **WHEN was the last time I used/wore it? AND, when is the next time I plan to use/wear it?**
Often we convince ourselves that we need to keep something because we might wear it again, but if you are really being honest with yourself, you know the likelihood is probably slim.

5) **WHY am I keeping it?**
GAME CHANGER!! I ask this of my clients all the time when they are on the fence about what to do. Are you keeping every piece of your kids' pre-K artwork because you feel like a bad mom if you throw it out? (Newsflash: You're not). Are you keeping

those jeans because you may fit into them someday? Guess what? If you get back down to a size 2, you deserve to buy yourself a new pair of jeans, so get rid of them!

Once you talk it through, you may find that you're not as attached as you originally thought.

People who can break free from the cycle of emotional clutter tend to feel a sense of relief. Once you give yourself the permission to let go, you will more than likely feel as though a giant weight has lifted off of you.

CHAPTER 6

Calendar Clutter

———

THE THIRD TYPE OF CLUTTER is what I like to call, calendar clutter: Trying to fit too many activities into too little time. If you've ever uttered the words "there just aren't enough hours in the day," chances are you suffer from calendar clutter.

Calendar clutter typically results from one of two things:

* Being overscheduled
* Poor time-management skills

BEING OVERSCHEDULED

Women are often pleasers by nature, so it's understandable that we frequently bite off more than we can chew.

Whether it's your boss adding additional responsibilities to your already full plate, or having to run from ballet to soccer to piano while also trying to cook dinner, we can feel as though we are being pulled in a million directions.

Any parent can tell you that coordinating everyone's schedules and chauffeuring kids around is like having an unpaid, thankless, full-time job.

Even if you don't have kids (or kids living at home), we need to take into account the time it takes to care for ailing parents, volunteer at events, or sit on committees. There is nothing wrong with doing a lot. Trust me, I am involved with plenty of things. The turning point is when you are so overextended, it starts to affect your ability to manage what is most important: Your life, home, and family.

Quick exercise: Think about your day like a closet. Now imagine filling it with some basic clothing and shoes. As time goes by, you accumulate more and more clothes and shoes, but refuse to get rid of anything. Your closet isn't getting any bigger, yet you continue to add more items, leaving less room for your clothing to breathe, and making it difficult to see what you have. Eventually, one of two things will happen: Either you will open the door, and everything will come falling down on you, or the load will get so heavy that the closet rod and shelves collapse.

Your calendar is no different. We need to make time and space in our schedule for what matters—in this case, reducing clutter in our lives.

If we spend the majority of our time running from one activity to another, we won't find time to take care of things at home: Laundry, dishes, mail (you know, all the fun stuff!). If you don't carve out time for these mundane tasks, clutter can creep up on you. Like my mother used to say, "The laundry isn't going to wash itself!"

Poor Time-Management Skills

Have you ever run around like a lunatic all day, then sat down and thought, "What did I accomplish today? I know I was busy, but I couldn't tell you what I did!" That, my friend, is an example of poor time management.

On the flip side, have you ever looked at someone and thought, "How does she get it all done?" You're not looking at Superwoman; you're looking at someone who knows how to maximize her time.

YOU can be that person. All you need to do is implement some simple strategies in your life and routine.

I'm not going to lie. Some people are naturally more organized with their time than others. My one daughter can successfully juggle playing varsity sports with carrying an intense workload; she gets everything done. My other daughter struggles with prioritizing assignments and often loses track of time. They are both smart, well-rounded individuals, but for one, time management comes naturally, while the other has to work on it. The good news is that with discipline, routine, and some simple strategies, you can learn to avoid time traps and accomplish what you want.

You may be wondering, what does my ability to manage my time have to do with clutter? If you are not efficient with your time, you will likely also be unable to effectively manage taking care of your home, your personal life, your kids, and your career. There just aren't enough hours in the day.

In the coming pages, I am going to talk about some simple strategies to help even the most disorganized people stay on task and remove calendar clutter from their lives.

––––

Five Tips for Conquering Calendar Clutter:

1) **Time block**. Have you ever kept a food journal? I have, and frankly it's one of the most tedious (yet telling) exercises I've ever done. Basically, you write down every morsel of food you put in your mouth each day. If you want to see change, you need to be honest about all those quick dips into the candy bowl, or finishing your child's chicken nuggets, because those calories add up. Time blocking is like a food diary for your daily activities. We tend to forget, or leave out, the little things we do that take up our time, such as driving to and from work, picking up the dry cleaning, or helping with homework. Time blocking forces you to account for every waking minute of your day, from the time you wake up until the time you go to bed. Once you write it all down, you can see how you're really spending your time, which activities take the most time, and which

tasks regularly fall to the back burner because there is not enough room in your schedule to get them done. From there, you can move to step 2.

2) **Prioritize your top-three tasks.** Do you have a never-ending to-do list? Between work, family, doctors appointments, shopping … our lists keep getting longer and longer. It seems as though every time I cross something off, another three things appear! Here's something I started doing several years ago that was another game changer for me. Every day, I prioritize three tasks that I need to accomplish. They are nonnegotiable and not part of my everyday responsibilities (such as taking the kids to school, making the bed, or cooking dinner). The tasks can be anything else—calling to schedule an overdue dentist appointment, paying the bills, or sitting down to clear my desk. Whatever three tasks I choose are a must; I prioritize them above everything else. Life is full of distractions, but we can't allow ourselves to get sidetracked each time something new pops up, otherwise we would never get anything done. Once you begin to focus on your top-three tasks, you should notice an increase in your efficiency and productivity.

3) **Work in manageable increments**. Somewhere along the way, we all started believing that everything we do needs to be epic. We can't just go out for a jog; we need to train for a race. We can't just eat healthily;

we need to lose weight. Don't get me wrong, I am all about setting goals, but let's just make them achievable. If you have 20 minutes to work out, it's better than nothing. If you have 10 minutes to read before the kids get off the bus, do it. I hear so many people say there isn't enough time to do the things they want to do, and my answer is that you need to *make* time. Even if it's not as much as you would like, a little bit goes a long way.

4) **Relinquish control**. All you control freaks out there, listen up! This one's for you. Until you learn to delegate and let go, you are limiting what you are capable of accomplishing. There are certain things that only an adult can do, especially if you have young kids at home (for example, cook a meal or drive to the store), but there are many areas where your family can (and should) be pitching in. Making the bed, setting and clearing the table, picking up toys, putting away laundry—these are all examples of household tasks that even young kids can do. This rule can apply to spouses as well. If your significant other doesn't fold the laundry the way you do, it doesn't mean it's wrong. The more you empower others to take things off your plate, the more time you have to focus on what you need to do. As a result, you should feel less overwhelmed.

5) **Use timesaving apps.** Many of my clients are tech-phobic, but like it or not, we live in a technological world. There are so many productivity apps out there; it's often difficult to choose what works best. I have spent years testing various apps, and I am going to share two of my favorites with you. That's not to say these are the only productivity apps you should be using, but they are the ones I found work best for my needs.

* Wunderlist is a list-making app that allows you to create simple to-do lists at any time, from any device. Whether you do all of your work from your iPhone, or spend most of your day behind a desktop computer, Wunderlist syncs wirelessly across your devices so you can update and share in real time. Instead of having one long to-do list, I create separate lists for home, kids, work, volunteering, and so on. This not only helps keep me from getting overwhelmed, but also allows me to choose one or two items from each list to complete each day. I share our household list with my husband so he can edit and update them too. I've been using Wunderlist for years and find it to be the easiest list app to navigate—especially if you are tech-phobic.

* The other app I use daily is Evernote. Evernote is a virtual notebook that allows you to easily create, share, and search notes. I use Evernote for

all of my client work, presentations, and article ideas. I have everything I need with me all the time in one central location. The best part about Evernote is twofold: eliminating paper clutter AND saving time. No more looking through stacks of notes to find what I need. All I have to do is key in a word in the search bar, and my note pops up. Plus it syncs wirelessly, so it's updated on my computer and phone simultaneously. I don't know what I would do without it. Evernote is a must-have!!!

CHAPTER 7

Digital Clutter

I WOULD BE REMISS IF I didn't at least touch on what I like to refer to as "the hidden clutter" known as digital clutter, which is often an extension of calendar clutter.

Digital clutter can range from having an unmanageable inbox to keeping thousands of photos on your camera roll. Twenty years ago, digital clutter didn't even exist, and today I have an entire workshop dedicated to helping people complete a digital detox.

Truth be told, I could write an entire book about digital clutter (and maybe I will—Hint! Hint!), but for now, I'm going to focus on a few areas where most of us seem to get sucked in.

FOUR TIPS FOR DEALING WITH DIGITAL CLUTTER:

1) **Set boundaries.** For better or worse, we live in a 24/7 global society where people are accessible at

least three ways, none of which involves picking up a phone. Between email, social media, and texting, people try to get our attention all the time. Most of us allow notifications of these messages to appear on our phones and computers, and we have become conditioned to responding as soon as we hear or see them. The first thing I want you to do when you put this book down is to pick up your smart phone and turn off push notifications. (If you're not sure how to do this on your particular device, just Google "how do I turn off notifications" and the type of device you have.) I also recommend doing this for email on your computer.

This will not only save battery life, but more importantly, it will allow *you* to control when you want to check social media and email. You will no longer be distracted by constant updates of who checked in where or commented on your status update.

I recommend checking email and social media only at certain times of day. Depending on your schedule, you can determine if it makes sense to do it first thing in the morning, during a midday break, or in the evening after everything settles down. If you're not disciplined enough to do this on your own, some great apps can help do this for you. One of my friends, Neen James, who just happens to be a worldwide productivity expert, turned me onto the app, <u>Freedom</u>, which allows you to set timers for accessing various social media sites. This may sound extreme to some of you, but it's so easy to get sucked into nonessential things that invade our time.

I can tell you, firsthand, that I am most productive on the days when I am on-site with clients and don't check my phone or laptop. I'm 100% focused on the task in front of me, and know my digital world will be waiting for me when I'm done. In the evening, I make time to read and respond to emails so I can go to bed without guilt.

2) **Treat your inbox like your closet.** The most organized closets are divided into categories so you know exactly where to find what you are looking for. Emails are no different. Creating email folders is a great way to retrieve things quickly. For example, I have a folder for each of my clients, my kids, and even travel. The more finely you separate categories, the easier it is to find what you are looking for, if you need to come back to it—which brings me to the next tip.

3) **Purge routinely.** This is where you grab a glass of wine, sit on the couch in front of some mindless TV, and clear out the clutter. The easiest way is to sort your emails by "from," then delete groups of emails with one click. Don't worry about trying to zero out your inbox. Even if you accomplish it, it's going to fill right back up. My best advice is to unsubscribe from

the newsletters (except mine of course ☺) and junk emails you never read. My other suggestion is to sign up for <u>unroll.me</u>, a service I use to help control email subscriptions. I talk about how it works in episode 21 of my podcast, *This ORGANIZED Life*, as well as why it's been a huge timesaver for me.

4) **Manage digital photos:** When it comes to digital photos, my best suggestion is to get them off of your phone or computer and onto a third-party site, like <u>Shutterfly, Dropbox,</u> or <u>Google Drive.</u> There are other services out there, but those are the ones I personally use. You don't have to be a tech expert; all of the sites I use are simple to navigate. The hardest part is getting over the fear that you don't know what you're doing.

Not managing your photos can cause problems for you. Too many people I know have lost photos permanently because they weren't backed up or put into the magical cloud. Have you ever tried to capture video of something, only to realize you don't have enough storage on your phone? How annoying is that? You find yourself standing there, feverishly deleting photos at random to create enough space. We've all been there. As with email, it's better to be proactive than waiting for that little popup box that says, "not enough storage."

The hardest part of this strategy is carving out time on the front end to do the initial setup. The upkeep is easy. Literally with the click of a button you can move photos from your phone to an album while waiting in the car pickup line at school.

To learn more, listen to episode 20 of my podcast, which is about organizing digital photos. I also have several articles on my blog about the topic, so be sure to check out those resources as well.

CHAPTER 8

Uncovering the Five Clutter Pitfalls

———

CLUTTER IS EXHAUSTING. IT NOT only makes us feel badly about our surroundings and ourselves, it also makes us physically tired.

I understand that sometimes it seems easier to avoid dealing with clutter and just go about our lives. Let's face it: We have plenty to do as it is. Who wants to deal with tackling that daunting task too?

Because behind our smiles and put-together exteriors lives a cycle of stress, anxiety, frustration, failure, chaos, and embarrassment. The million-dollar question is really: "If we know how badly our clutter makes us feel, why do we continue to keep it in our lives?"

There are lots of reasons we find ourselves in the "clutter boat," but I've narrowed it down to five. Let's take a look at the five clutter pitfalls and see if you can relate.

1) **Procrastination:** Let's be honest. There is always something else we can do besides daily chores. "I'll

The Five Clutter Pitfalls Model

get to it later" are famous last words. The problem arises when later becomes tomorrow, which turns into next week or next month, and before you know it, once-simple tasks like sorting mail and putting away laundry have turned into a weekend of decluttering.

2) **Indecision:** Have you ever thought to yourself, "I am not sure what to do with X so I'll put it over here for now"? Your intent isn't to create a mess; it just seems easier to do nothing than make a wrong choice. But that becomes a problem when you continually refrain from making decisions. Soon, you

can find yourself staring at an "I don't know where it goes" pile that has evolved into a mountain of clutter. Think about something as simple as a piece of mail—an invoice to be paid, an invitation that needs an RSVP, or an update on your insurance policy. These are classic examples of how indecision can turn a piece of paper into a pile of clutter. Assigning a home for everything (in other words, "here is where I put bills to be paid, here is where I file things") takes the guesswork out of where things belong.

3) **Guilt:** Putting too much emotional value on something is one of the most common reasons why clutter accumulates. Don't allow guilt to stand in the way of making a decision about what you keep in your home. We talk ourselves into believing that we will someday use this, or sell that, but rarely does that happen. Keeping a pile for later is just moving your clutter from one room to the next. If you aren't sure what to do with something, ask yourself "When is the next time I am going to use these cookie cutters? Or wear those leather pants?" If you don't have a concrete answer, it may be time to let it go. Regardless of how expensive your stuff was originally, it has no value sitting on a shelf or hanging in a closet. If you're not using it, maybe someone else can. If you are really struggling, I recommend giving yourself a deadline to use it, sell it, or donate it.

4) **Overwhelm:** When we walk into a space that is filled with clutter, our eyes don't know where to focus. Whether it's dishes in the sink, toys on the floor, or piles of paper on the counter, the thought of where to begin can be downright frightening. When those anxious feelings arise, it's tempting to shut the door and run away. There are lots of things in life we have limited control over, but fortunately clutter is not one of them. The good news is that you have a say in what enters and leaves your home and how things are organized. Stop letting your clutter control you and take control of your clutter. Reducing clutter reduces stress.

5) **Time:** We live in a society where we are all overscheduled, overworked, and overwhelmed. We barely have time to sit and eat a proper meal or get a good night's sleep, let alone sort clutter for hours. Time management is by far one of the most common obstacles we face. The good news is that once you develop a strategy and have a clear plan of action, you can designate a specific amount of time each day or week to addressing clutter. I always tell people, "your clutter didn't accumulate overnight, so don't expect it to disappear in a day. A little at a time is all you need to start seeing a difference."

You may relate to some, or even all, of the five clutter pitfalls. Identifying your personal roadblocks can help you understand the root of your clutter and begin to develop strategies that help you avoid falling into the same patterns. This is a great way to begin your journey to a more organized, less cluttered life.

My clutter pitfalls are: _____

**"Identify your problems, but give your
power and energy to solutions."**

—Tony Robbins

Part 2: Solutions

___

NOW THAT YOU UNDERSTAND THE origin of your clutter and can define it, it's time to learn some strategies to help you navigate through the de-cluttering and organizing process. I've designed the process to make it less daunting, and to be generic enough so you can apply it across various rooms and situations.

CHAPTER 9

When Is a Good Time to Get Organized?

———

RECENTLY, I WAS TALKING TO a friend of mine who has three young children between the ages of two and seven. She asked me, "So tell me, when is the best time for me to get organized?" I paused for a moment, thinking of how to best answer her, then decided to answer honestly: "What's wrong with today?"

She looked surprised and responded, "Really? With three little kids at home?"

I suppose it's how I define being organized. In my world, living an organized life isn't about having a perfect home. It's not about fancy custom closets or tossing all your childhood memories in the trash. In it's simplest form, it's about three things:

- ❧ Establishing a system that works for you.
- ❧ Ensuring all your belongings have a home.
- ❧ Maintaining the system easily.

Having a sense of organization in your life goes deeper than labeled bins on a shelf. Reducing clutter:

* Helps reduce unnecessary stress, frustration, chaos, and anxiety from your life.
* Improves self-esteem.
* Allows you to spend more time doing the things you want, with the people who mean the most to you.

Let's be honest, there is never an ideal time to get organized. Life is hectic. I know that as well as anyone. Undeniably, some periods of our lives are more demanding, which is all the more reason to get off the clutter train and get organized!

Sometimes all you need is someone to point you in the right direction, provide you with an alternative perspective, and most importantly, understand your struggle. **Being organized is not about perfection; it's about balance.**

Think about dieting. You want to lose weight, you have your plan, and you're ready to go. You have the best of intentions, and then reality gets in the way! Your boss is a jerk, your kids refuse to listen, and every time you start something, you get pulled away to some crisis only you can handle. The next thing you know, you're watching BRAVO, shoving a piece of birthday cake in your mouth.

We've all been there. It may be frustrating, but don't allow one roadblock to derail you. Instead of throwing your hands in the air and giving up, I encourage you to eat the cake! Remember, tomorrow is another day and a new opportunity for a fresh start.

You can apply the same philosophy to organizing. It is unrealistic to think your home will be organized 24/7, 365 days a year. I used to think that if I can't do something 100%, I shouldn't do it at all (a very common trait for "type A" folks like me). It finally clicked that 80% was better than 0%—a simple concept, yet it took me years of frustration and feelings of failure to finally grasp it!

Don't allow life to be the roadblock that keeps you from getting organized. Things will get hectic, and you will fall off-task, but having a system in place will allow you to get back on track effortlessly.

To answer my friend's question: "The best time to get organized is now."

CHAPTER 10

Knowing Your Peak Productivity Time

——

WHEN I SPEAK TO MY corporate clients, I talk a lot about maximizing their peak productivity time, but productivity is not something limited to the workplace.

I have never been a night owl. When growing up, I remember going to bed while my mom stayed up past midnight, folding laundry and watching TV. In college, my roommate, Aimee, stayed up until 3 AM cleaning (yes, cleaning!), while I slept soundly. I always preferred morning classes and could never pull an all-nighter.

Each of us has a time of day when we are at the top of our game. For some, it's early morning, for others midday, and still others are night owls. Trying to find a one-size-fits-all solution for the best time to embark on a project doesn't work.

When my older daughter first started school, she would get off the bus, have a snack, and immediately start her homework. That's what I always did as a kid, and it made sense that she would follow in my footsteps. I never really gave it much thought until my younger daughter started school. She would come off the bus utterly exhausted. It was a struggle to get her to unpack her backpack, let alone start her homework. Some days she would actually fall asleep within minutes of walking in the door. Naturally, I wanted her to get her homework done, not just for her sake, but also for mine. I fought with her to sit down and do it immediately. I never took into account that she had ADHD and needed to decompress after sitting in school all day. Homework that should have taken 30 minutes was taking upward of two hours.

After months of battles and tears (hers, not mine—I preferred wine), I finally had my light-bulb moment: I realized she goes into a valley in the afternoon. I never factored in her peak productivity time, only mine. I discovered that if I gave her time to chill out and relax for an hour first, she would come back more focused and less combative.

We all know when we are at our best, and when we are basically just going through the motions. Decluttering and organizing require both mental and physical strength, so being cognizant of your peak productivity time (and that of those around you) is an important part of the process.

If you are a morning person, consider carving out an hour or two once a week to stay home and play catch up. If you are a night owl, pick one night a week after the kids go to bed to check something off your to-do list. Try to tackle the chores you like least when you are most productive, and leave the mundane for when you are more relaxed (folding laundry, for example). Some things require brainpower and others are mindless, so choose wisely. Sometimes there is no good time, but it's better to "rip the Band-Aid off" and do it than leave it hanging over your head.

CHAPTER 11

What Is Your Organizational Style?

―――

ONCE YOU'VE IDENTIFIED THE DOMINANT cause of your clutter (physical, emotional, or calendar) and your peak productivity times, ask yourself some questions about your **organizational style**.

You may be thinking: "What the heck is my organizational style?" Even if you've never analyzed your behavior and habits, you have a preferred organizational style. (Remember Susan from Chapter 4?) Let's find out what yours is.

There are two main types of organizational styles:

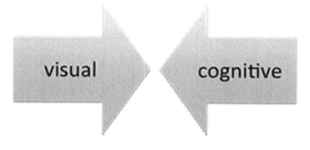

Organizational Style Model

1) **Visual** people are more productive when they see what's in front of them. They often fall into the "out of sight, out of mind" mentality. As a result, they often leave things out so they don't forget. Problems arise when these physical reminders end up as clutter. To be productive, visual people tend to work better with the use of whiteboards, pin boards, letterboxes, and clear, labeled bins. They also prefer open shelving or cubbies to closet cabinetry.

2) **Cognitive** folks prefer to have everything behind closed doors. They don't want to see anything. These people tend to rely on memory, which can become an issue if they are not diligent about putting things back in their designated spaces. I've seen cognitive people shove things in drawers, cabinets, or closets, simply to avoid seeing them. They tend to prefer closed cabinetry to open shelving and can benefit from drawer dividers, defined filing systems, and electronic or digital options rather than paper.

If you're unsure of your organizational style, take this quick quiz:

1) I don't like anything on my counters. *True or False*

2) I use Post-it notes for to-do lists and important information. *True or False*

3) I store my tasks and information on my phone or computer. *True or False*

4) My dream is to have a ROYGBIV closet. *True or False*

5) I get all my bills online. *True or False*

6) I often buy things I already own because I forgot I had them. *True or False*

7) I don't like to see toys out, even if they're neatly organized. *True or False*

8) I prefer to hang my clothes rather than folding them. *True or False*

9) As long as I don't see it, it doesn't bother me. *True or False*

10) I use a whiteboard or large calendar to remind me of what's going on. *True or False*

Scoring: Marking more odd-numbered questions "true" indicates a cognitive style, while marking more even-numbered questions "true" suggests a visual style.

Okay, great. What does that mean? As you begin to think about the daunting task of organizing, you want to factor in your style and habits to determine what will work and what won't.

For instance, designing a space with open shelving for someone who doesn't like to see his or her stuff is not going to work. Instead, you might want to consider using closed cabinetry. Likewise, if you are constantly forgetting things, I recommend posting a checklist somewhere apparent as a visual reminder of everything you need to do that doesn't rely on memory (this is great for kids!). Keep in mind; there are various ways to get creative, and it may require some trial and error before you find the system that works best for you.

CHAPTER 12

Where Do I Begin?

————

Now that you've made the commitment to getting started, the question of "Where do I begin?" usually follows. Knowing where to start is a big issue for many. The advice I always give my clients is to start with the room or space that causes you the most stress.

* If it stresses you out that your entry way looks like a dumping ground, and that's the first thing you see when you walk in the door, start there.

* If your home office is littered with paper clutter, bills are past due, and you feel anxious before you sit down, prioritizing your office might be a good place to start.

* If you keep buying the same spices over and over because no rhyme or reason governs the order of your kitchen, then I'd say that is a great place to start.

Focusing on your biggest pain point, rather than attempting to declutter your entire house in a weekend, is a much more realistic approach.

Seeing one project through to completion is harder than it seems. How often do you start something only to get sucked into doing something else? You know it's a problem when you have started half dozen projects, but have completed none. Sound familiar?

Working within a defined area allows you to easily see the light at the end of the tunnel and keeps you motivated. Most importantly, you are less likely to feel overwhelmed and have the "what have I gotten myself into" thought midway through the project. You should only declutter the next space on your list after you've completed the first project.

CHAPTER 13

Organizational ESP

THE GREAT THING ABOUT ORGANIZING is that, regardless of the room you choose to declutter, there are basic organizing principles you can apply across the board. Life gets complicated, so everything I teach is based on the foundation of *simplicity*. I developed what I call **organizational ESP**, which is a basic three-step process to get you started on the path to organization.

Organizational ESP Model

Step 1: Empty. Before you can organize any space, you need to see what you have. What better way to do that than to empty it? Let's use the good old junk drawer as an example. The first thing I suggest is to clear a workspace, such as a counter or the floor, then spread the contents out and get down to it. That's step one: Empty all the contents. I know that sounds overwhelming, but it's incredibly difficult to organize a space in the midst of all that clutter. Removing it gives you a blank canvas to work with.

Tip: When you start this process, choose *small* areas. Don't attempt to empty the basement all at once unless you have a solid plan, a lot of time, and some help!

Step 2: Sort. Once everything has been emptied, you can group like items into piles—all pencils, paper clips, notepads, and so on. As you do, move things to four piles as follows: KEEP, DONATE, RECYCLE, and RELOCATE.

In other words, ask yourself four basic questions about each item:

- Is this something I want to keep?
- Is this something I want to donate?

- Is this something that can be recycled or needs to be thrown away?
- Is this something I want to keep, but belongs in a different place?

Tip: Don't think too long about your answers. In the beginning, if you follow your natural instincts, your "keep" pile may be larger than the rest. Look at each item for only a few seconds and try to determine which pile it belongs in. If you are really stuck on something, pass and move on to the next item.

- **Pile 1: Keep.** If you choose to place something in the keep pile, ask yourself the follow-up question, "Why?" Think back to the three main types of clutter and the five clutter pitfalls, and challenge your motivation for holding onto something. By rule of thumb, if you are currently using it, wearing it, or playing with it, it should remain in the keep pile; otherwise it belongs in one of the other three piles.
- **Pile 2: Donate.** This happens to be my favorite pile. Any opportunity I find to help someone less fortunate than I am makes me happy. Helping others is a value my husband and I also instill in our girls. Anytime we no longer use something, whether it's clothing, toys, or household items, we pay it forward. I talk more about places to donate in my resources section. As you sort your stuff, just keep this thought

in mind: "If it's in good condition but I don't use it, wouldn't it be better to allow someone else to enjoy and benefit from it, than to let it sit on a shelf or in a drawer?" (Hint: Is this emotional clutter?)

* **Pile 3: Recycle.** I use the word recycling refer to any kind of trash. As much as I love to donate items, some things are just not worthy. Items that are broken, stained, torn, or damaged beyond repair should all go into the recycling bin. Unfortunately, outdated electronic equipment and televisions can fall into this category. I am all about being mindful of the environment and disposing of things properly. So I encourage you to call your municipal office or to Google "electronics recycling near me" to find a place to dispose of outdated electronics properly. Some communities have a bulk-recycling day—a great option for keeping your basement, attic, or garage from looking like a junkyard.

* **Pile 4: Relocate.** This pile is often overlooked, but is equally important as the other three. These are things you want to keep, but not in the current spot. For example, if you are cleaning your pantry and come across one of your kid's toys, you may want to keep it, but clearly not in the pantry. The toy would go in the relocate pile, which means the next time you walk to the toy area, you will put that toy where it belongs. The same holds true for keepsakes. There may be things you want to hold onto, like your child's first shoes or your old

varsity jacket. There is a place for those items; it's called "memorabilia storage" (and we cover that in a later chapter). For now, just move them out of your "prime real estate."

Now that you have sorted your things into four piles, you should be left with a fraction of what you started with, making organizing the "keep" pile a manageable organizational task. I cover how to reorganize those items in the next chapter.

Side note: *I sometimes make an additional pile, called Sell for things of value I think I can sell or consign. However, I try to avoid this as much as possible, mainly because it's time consuming, doesn't typically result in a high return on investment, and often distracts from the task at hand.*

Step 3: Purge. Purging refers to anything that you no longer need or want to keep. When I say an item is going to be purged, I typically mean that it can be recycled or thrown away. In actuality, you started the purge process as you navigated through the four piles. The important part of the purge is to actually remove the items from the house before someone decides to put them back. I've walked into plenty of homes with bags in a corner where people have said to me "those are for donation," but you haven't completed the purge process until you remove the items entirely from your space.

At first, the purge pile may seem overwhelming, but as you continue to repeat the process, that feeling of being overwhelmed should slowly transition to a sense of freedom. You may not see it right now, but you can trust me on this one.

Congratulations! You have just mastered organizational ESP.

CHAPTER 14

Zoning, Layout, & Labeling

———

Now that you have ESP'd a space in your home, you should know what items you need to organize. The next step is to figure out how to make that space more functional. When you think about organizing your space—regardless of whether it's a garage, kitchen, or closet—think not only about how you use it now, but more importantly, how you WANT to use it. Based on your contents, what categories are critical to keeping your items organized? I believe this is a pivotal part of the process, and the one that gets overlooked the most. **Developing a well thought out strategy requires research, thought and patience.** Below are a few examples of questions you may want to ask yourself before you get started.

KITCHEN QUESTIONS	CLOSET QUESTIONS	GARAGE QUESTIONS
Do you like to bake?	Do you like to fold or hang?	How many cars do you want to park inside?
Do you shop in bulk?	How many categories of clothing do you have?	How much do you want to invest in products?
How often do you entertain?	Do you prefer to see things or have them behind closet doors?	How many kinds of items do you need to organize? (e.g., sports, gardening, tools, seasonal)

These are just a few examples of questions you'll want to answer before you get started. It can seem overwhelming. You may not have all the answers, but asking these questions will save you time and money down the road.

ZONING

In the simplest of terms, zoning is the process of keeping similar items together. For example: Zoning a garage would mean keeping all tools in one area, gardening supplies in another, sports equipment in a third, and so on.

It sounds like a basic concept, but you would be amazed at how many people don't do this. If your garage is a jumbled mess of WD-40, Raid, and a ball pump, don't feel bad—you're in good company!

First things first: There is no right way to zone a room. I wish I could tell you that there is a one-size-fits-all template for zoning a space, but there is not. Different spaces require different methods, based on convenience.

Generally speaking, the most popular way is to zone by category: All gardening supplies together, all tools together, and so on. However sometimes it makes more sense to zone by person: A bin for each child, a bin for your spouse, and a bin for you. This is especially helpful in mudrooms or entryways where you are storing things like gloves, mittens, and hats, and you want each person to easily identify their belongings. Other times, you may want to zone by color. This is a particularly popular method if you're organizing a bedroom closet; I call this the ROYGBIV method (red, orange, yellow, green, blue, violet). I know for me, it's much easier to get dressed in the morning when I can go over to my black shirts and select the one I want, as opposed to rifling through a sea of randomly mixed clothes. When it comes to developing a filing system, zoning is critical since all papers look alike. I find the easiest way to zone files is alphabetically. Regardless of your preferences, the key takeaway is that the system you choose should be easy to follow, make sense for you and your family, and make maintaining order simple.

One of the most productive ways to reduce stress and reclaim time is by grouping like items together. Imagine how much time you'll save when you go to look for something and actually know where it is! How many times have you grabbed a flashlight that needed batteries and gone searching through drawers in the dark to find them? How about something as simple as keeping all your chargers and headphones in one place, rather than wasting time searching all over the house because there's no defined home for them? It may sound like common sense to you, but you would be amazed at how many people don't place value in the details.

Sometimes it's easier to write down your categories first. I find this helpful when I'm organizing closets and kitchens. In a kitchen you might have categories like: baking supplies, canned goods, pasta and grains, snacks. In a closet you would have categories such as: pants, sweaters, long-sleeve shirts, dresses, work clothes. However, in larger spaces that have gotten way out of control with clutter, you may have to dig in first, even to assess what the heck you have. This often happens in rooms like garages, playrooms, or offices.

Either way, keep it simple. I've seen clients overcomplicate the process by making too many categories. That fine grain of detail may sound good, but requires a lot of time and effort to maintain.

———

LAYOUT

Once you've established which zones you need, it's time to focus on the best layout for your needs.

Whether you are designing a room from scratch or working within a challenging existing space, the first thing I ask people is to think about the key factors that will make your life easier:

* Which items do you need within reach?
* Which do you need to access frequently?
* Who is using the space?
* What is his or her organizational style (cognitive or visual)?
* Is height a factor for anyone?
* What can be relocated to other areas or removed altogether?

Once you've answered these questions, you will begin developing a roadmap of where things should go.

Think in terms of maximizing your **prime real estate.**

Prime real estate is the area of a room that is used most often, highly trafficked, and rarely sufficient in terms of space. For me, I struggled to create storage space in my mudroom for backpacks, coats, and sweatshirts. For some, pantries or kitchen cabinets are the prime real estate challenge.

If you think of your space in terms of prime real estate, you want to make sure the items you routinely use are front and center. The rest can (and should) be relocated, or in many cases, removed all together.

Things you use only once or twice a year—such as seasonal items or that turkey platter you only use on Thanksgiving— should be reserved for higher shelves, or better yet, a separate area like a basement, garage, or attic, since you access them infrequently.

One of the biggest mistakes people make is designing a layout based on style rather than function. Let me tell you about one of my clients and you'll have a better understanding of what I'm talking about:

True story: A woman hired me to help her organize her kitchen. When I walked into the space, I was greeted by a beautiful, open concept, recently renovated kitchen. It was equipped with a spacious island, beautiful cabinetry, and lots of storage space. At first glace, I was perplexed as to why she felt the need to call me, but as we navigated through the kitchen it was evident why she was frustrated: Her kitchen had a poor layout.

This busy mom of three young children was constantly scrambling to find what she needed. She was wasting time running all over her kitchen looking for things that should have been at her fingertips. Anyone who has kids knows the importance of convenience; being able to reach things quickly can mean the difference between chaos and calm. She turned to me and said: "I made the mistake of designing the kitchen I wanted versus the kitchen I needed."

When designing her dream kitchen, my client selected the cabinets she liked and the countertops she wanted, but she never took the time to think through the best layout for how she and her family functioned.

It took me no more than 10 minutes to establish what I would have done differently. I would have placed drawers where there was a cabinet. I would have flipped her island so that her kids could use it as a homework and snack area while she was preparing dinner. And I would have incorporated rollout shelving in her pantry so items didn't get lost in the back.

Unfortunately, unless she was prepared to make some expensive changes, it was too late to give her the kitchen of her dreams. Nonetheless, we were able to rezone the room and make it functional.

I started by corralling her kids' snacks into bins so that open bags and boxes didn't litter her pantry shelves. I clearly labeled these and made them accessible to the kids, so they could find what they needed independently.

Then I moved items that she used infrequently, like her Kitchen-Aid mixer, to a corner cabinet, rather than keeping it on her island—an area I consider prime real estate. By opening up that space, I was able to move her Tupperware containers from the corner cabinet to within easy reach. Considering she uses her mixer only once or twice a year, it made more sense to occupy that prime real estate with something she uses on a daily basis.

I collected all of their water bottles in a bin so they wouldn't topple over every time someone opened the cabinet. And some simple and inexpensive dividers put the finishing touches inside her drawers. Not only did they look custom-made, but they prevented things from getting lost in an otherwise jumbled mess.

Overall, these tweaks didn't cost a lot, but they helped make her day-to-day life less hectic and the kitchen more functional, not only for her but for the kids as well. The moral of my story is this: **Pretty doesn't always mean functional. Think of your needs first and the aesthetics will follow.** An efficient layout doesn't have to cost a fortune. Investing in some shelving, organizational systems, or assorted bins and baskets to maximize your space may provide a simple fix.

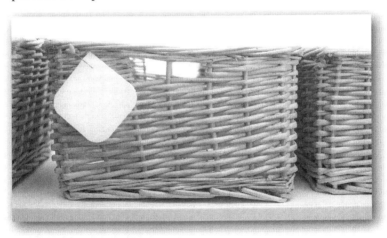

Depending on your budget, there are various options out there. I've helped people get creative with a hammer and nails to hang gardening supplies and sports equipment, and I've customized entire renovations with clients' specific space and contents in mind. The majority of people fall somewhere in the middle of these extremes and select versatile options that adapt well with their family's evolving needs.

Some organizing must-haves:

- **Drawer dividers:** To keep categories separate and avoid multiple junk drawers
- **Open bins and baskets:** To store anything from snacks in the kitchen, to action figures or LEGOS in the playroom, to gloves and mittens in the closet
- **Clear latched bins in various sizes:** To organize light bulbs, seasonal decorations, memorabilia, or off-season clothes
- **Label maker or removable write-on labels:** To easily identify contents

Just remember that as your needs grow, you will want to have some versatility within your space to adapt to those changes. For example, when my kids were younger, I used to have plastic plates and cups on a rollout shelf in my island, which made it easy for my girls to set the table. Was this the ideal spot? At the time, yes, because I wanted them to be able to help out. But once they got older and taller, I was able to donate those plastic plates, which opened up the space for other things.

Layout can prove challenging to people who rent and are not permitted to install permanent systems in their current spaces. One of my New York clients had a temporary wall put up in her daughters' shared room to give each child their own separate space!

For people in apartments, maximizing storage is key. Under-bed storage can make a bed double as a dresser. Coffee and end tables that open or have shelving are great for storing extra blankets, books, or photo albums. Standalone closet systems, like the IKEA PAX series, look like built-ins but can easily be taken with you when you move.

Whether this is your forever home or a short-term rental, your layout should be efficient, fluid, and adaptable, just like life.

———

LABELING

From a functional perspective, labeling is a way to easily identify the contents of a given space, removing the guesswork out of wondering what's inside your bins, baskets, and drawers.

From a style perspective, labels add character, warmth, and a personal touch to your belongings. It is the finishing touch that often gets overlooked.

Now that you've worked to empty, sort, purge, and zone your space, think of labels as the icing on the cake or the cherry on your sundae.

My one suggestion is that you invest in a label maker. You can find a fairly inexpensive, quality label maker at most office supply stores or online. I actually just had to replace mine after about 15 years and only spent $34.99. They are easy to use and somewhat addicting!

Here are some examples of how I use my label maker throughout the house:

* In my pantry, I use it to label bins for snacks, pasta, cereal bars, crackers, baking supplies, and more; the list is endless. Labels are critical for visual folks because you can identify your contents in a snap.
* In my mudroom, I have separate bins of different-sized batteries and each one is labeled: AA, AAA, D, C, 9V. Not only does this allow me find them easily, but I know when I am running low and need to replenish. There is nothing more annoying than not having a battery when you need one.
* In the garage, I label everything from my light bulb bin to seasonal decorations.

If you want to get creative, there are countless templates available online that you can download, print, and use to label spices, toys, or anything in between. You can also label things by color or picture, which is great for little ones who haven't learned how to read. Often, when organizing a playroom, we label bins with words and pictures to make it easy for kids to know what belongs where (e.g., trucks, blocks, and so on).

The great thing about most labels is that you can interchange them with your needs. What may have once served to store LEGOS® may now be used for video games. I am constantly switching out bins—which is the beauty of versatile storage that adapts to your needs.

Side note: *When my youngest was in elementary school, she was obsessed with my label maker. I will never forget, when she was in second grade, she asked to borrow it and put the following label on her folder: "People who give me headaches." Inside was a list of names. Clearly, her labeling obsession knows no boundaries.*

CHAPTER 15

Plan First, Buy Later

———

HAVE YOU EVER BOUGHT A bunch of cool organizing products that you saw online, on TV, or in a store, and thought: "That will help get me organized!" Only once you get it home do you realize it was not the right size, didn't fit your space, or didn't help you do what you wanted to do?

Talk about a buzzkill. Not only is your clutter still here, but you've spent money on a new product that will more than likely be added to your existing clutter. A lose-lose situation!

WORD TO THE WISE: PLAN FIRST, BUY LATER.

Believe me, I've stood on line at Bed Bath & Beyond and seen the supposed "latest and greatest cure for your clutter" and also thought: "This is going to solve my problem!"

Guess what? The "cure" to your clutter isn't on the end-cap at Bed Bath & Beyond. You'll find it by creating a system that you and your family can follow.

Here's a good illustration of the value of planning before you buy:

True story: *A friend of mine has four active kids, all with a lot of stuff. Over the course of several years, her two-car garage became the dumping ground for bikes, sporting equipment, camping gear, and everything in between—except her cars. Until this point, she believed that clutter was her only option. With an active family of six, what choice did she have?*

Although she had resigned herself to a disorganized life, there was one problem: The family was getting ready to put their house on the market. My friend realized she wouldn't be able to sell her house with the garage in its current state. She was completely overwhelmed. Not knowing where to begin, she did the right thing: She called me.

The first thing I did after I looked at the garage was talk with her. I needed to find out what she wanted the space to look like and how she needed it to function. Did she want the ability to park both cars inside? One car? No cars? Did she need an area for sports equipment? Bikes? Cleaning Supplies? Tools? Each of these unique items needs to have its own zone, and her answers would give me an idea of how much room I had to work with. All she kept saying was, "What do I need to buy?" She thought products would solve her problem. But until I saw what was in her keep pile, I couldn't tell her what the best options were. Purchasing was premature.

Planning is great, but you can only tell what products are best for your space after you go through your Organizational ESP and truly know the volume of stuff you need to organize. Too many people buy things they don't need and wind up wasting time and money on the wrong products. By being patient and navigating the decluttering process first, will you know what you need to purchase.

Hence: Plan first, buy later.

The top-selling product from the Container Store won't do the trick if you are still surrounded by clutter.

Tip: People often overlook things they already own. Before you buy anything, look around your home for items that you have. Things like buckets, baskets, pitchers, or Mason jars make great organizing tools. Repurposing not only saves money, but it allows your personal style to be reflected in your space.

CHAPTER 16

Memorabilia Storage

———

A BIG MISCONCEPTION THAT MANY people have about professional organizers is that we want you to throw everything out. Of course, I can only speak for myself, but I assure you that is not the case. As I said earlier, my goal is not to convert you to a minimalist. Nor do I want to erase any physical memories you own.

As a matter of fact, I will be the first person to tell you that everyone should hold onto keepsakes that have sentimental meaning. Memorabilia is a personal snapshot of your past. It could be a varsity jacket, photos from college, sketchbooks, or anything else you want to hold onto. Whatever mementos you deem important are worth keeping—plain and simple. How and where you store them are where I come into play.

When it comes to memorabilia, one of the most common things I see is that people don't know what to do with these items. Where should I keep them? How should I store them? What products should I use for them? These questions often paralyze us from moving forward.

As we talked about earlier, when people are uncertain of what to do with something, they often do nothing (think back to the five clutter pitfalls). As a result, there is often no rhyme or reason for where things are kept: Photos are shoved in drawers and old clothing is kept in a closet, even though you have no intention of ever wearing it, expect maybe for a Halloween costume.

So where do these keepsakes belong? Just like a hammer belongs with tools, your keepsakes belong in your memorabilia storage. Think of it as a home for your memories. Having these items stored in one place reduces clutter, protects them from getting lost or damaged, and makes retrieval easy if you ever want to take a walk down memory lane.

There are different types of memorabilia storage for various items. I always recommend having one memory box easily accessible for cards, ticket stubs, or letters. I like to keep mine on the top shelf of my closet. I also recommend having one large memory bin of keepsakes per person. I like clear, lidded, and latched Sterilite bins for this purpose. Some of you may be shaking your heads, thinking, "There's no way can I cram my entire youth into one 70-quart storage container!" If you feel like you need more, so be it.

Just be mindful and ask yourself why you are keeping each item. As we touched upon when talking about emotional clutter, it's important to understand why you feel the need to keep things.

I see parents fall into this trap all the time, especially when it comes to holding onto their kids' homework. Not every scrap of paper your child scribbled on is worth saving. I'm sure I'm getting dirty looks out the wazoo right now. Asking parents to decide which of their kids' projects to keep and which to toss is as difficult as asking them to choose between a headache and an upset stomach.

If you feel as though I am talking directly to you, I've designed a little cheat-sheet to help get you over the mountain of parental guilt:

- Does it have your child's handprint? **Keep.**
- Is it a sticker project that anyone could have done? **Toss.**
- Does it tell a story (e.g., a family vacation, a self-portrait)? **Keep.**
- Is it a bunch of glued-on cutouts a teacher gave your kid? **Toss.**
- Is it one of the first times your child wrote his or her name? **Keep.**
- Is it an addition or subtraction practice sheet? **Toss.**

Once you begin, you'll more than likely be surprised at how painless the process can be. Thanks to technology, you can also keep digital copies of your kids' artwork. There is a great app called <u>ArtKive</u> that allows you to easily snap a picture with your phone and upload it to a digital album that can be printed into a book. You can make one for each school year and event print a copy for the grandparents!

Tip: When it comes to navigating kids' homework, I suggest going through it each day, just like the mail. As your kids get older, you can do it together and allow them to assess what goes in the keep and recycle piles.

As you are deciding whether something is memorabilia-worthy, keep the why in mind. Why am I keeping this? Do I love it? Do I want to pass it along to my kids when they grow up? Do I feel guilty for getting rid of it? If so, how come? Don't allow memorabilia to mask your emotional clutter. Keepsakes are a wonderful way to honor our memories, but it's the art of being selective that separates what truly holds value from what you can donate or purge.

True story: When my mom died in 2011, I inherited all of her Christmas ornaments, including her snowman collection (my mom LOVED snowmen!). So in addition to my own Christmas decorations, I now had another eight tubs of ornaments and decorations. I loved my mom and was happy to be able to display a part of her collection in my home—it was like a part of her was still with us. However, truth be told, I didn't love all of her stuff, some items were similar to what I already owned, and frankly, I didn't have room to keep everything.

I chose to keep her snowman collection and a few special ornaments, and to donate the rest. I condensed everything I wanted to keep from eight bins to two, so I didn't have to worry about creating new space in my garage. More importantly, because I was selective, I was able to create a special "Nana" section to honor her traditions and memory. Someday, my girls will inherit these and do what they want with them—without feeling guilty or overwhelmed. I felt good donating the remaining items. There was no need for them to sit on a shelf in my garage. I'd rather they bring joy to someone, and I know that's what my mother would have wanted too.

CHAPTER 17

Overflow Storage

———

IN A WORLD OF BULK shopping, I'd be remiss if I didn't include a chapter on overflow storage. Our cabinets weren't designed to hold 48 rolls of toilet paper, 12 cans of spaghetti sauce, and a case of macaroni and cheese. There's nothing wrong with stocking up on things that you will use, but it's important to designate a separate space for what doesn't fit in your cabinets. One of the biggest frustrations I see is when my clients try to cram these items into their living space rather than do this.

What does a proper overflow storage area look like? The good thing about overflow storage is that the primary goal is functionality. Basic wood shelving or wire bakers racks are great places to store bulk items. Picture the shelving at BJ's, Costco, or Sam's Club.

You want your overflow area to be nearby, since you'll need to access it frequently to replenish your stash. Garages, unfinished storage areas in the basement, or even spare closets can act as great overflow areas. I've even seen people turn wasted space under the stairs into functional storage equipped with shelving and lighting.

Speaking of lighting, you want to make sure that your overflow storage area is well lit so you can see what's there! I don't recommend spending a lot of money on bins because most bulk items, like granola bars and other snacks, comes in their own packaging. As long as everything is elevated off the floor, zoned by category, and packaged, you should be fine.

True story: When we lived in our first house, we had no pantry and limited cabinet space. Fortunately, our basement was right off the kitchen so we created a walk-in closet with simple wood shelving to act as overflow storage. It was nothing worthy of Pinterest by any stretch of the imagination, but it allowed me to keep my kitchen clutter-free.

If you like to stock up on paper products, canned goods, or snacks, designating an overflow area that is separate from your main living space can help you be organized about it.

CHAPTER 18

Getting the Kids Involved

———

As parents, we all want what's best for our kids. We want them to grow up to be intelligent, educated, talented, kind, caring, compassionate individuals who are contributing members of society. If you also want to help your child become independent, responsible, and self-reliant, which I'm going to assume we all do, one of the most important things you can do is to empower them to get involved with the organizing process.

Here are five tips for getting the family on board:

1) **Teach them while they're young.** Imagine you want to learn a foreign language as an adult. It's doable, but it takes tremendous effort and practice to become fluent. Now think about a child who is raised bilingual: They can speak both languages without thinking twice. Children's brains are like sponges, absorbing knowledge of all kinds, whether it's academics, music, language, athletics, or life skills. The key is

setting age-appropriate goals. For instance, it's perfectly acceptable to ask a one-year old to put a book back on the bookshelf after reading it, or to teach a five-year-old to pull up the covers after getting out of bed. As they grow and mature, you can gradually add responsibilities they can handle.

2) **Speak their language.** When it comes to working with kids, you need to speak their language and make tasks relevant to them. Be specific in your instructions. Avoid general statements like "Clean your room," because to them, that may mean shoving everything under the bed or in the closet. Instead say, "I want you to pick up your dirty clothes from the floor and put them in the hamper." Or, "Please put all of your toys in the bin." I'm not saying it's easy, but if you incorporate these strategies into their responsibilities, like brushing their teeth, they will eventually become second nature.

3) **Make it fun.** Who says organizing has to be boring? Here is a game I call Race Against the Clock: Take one basket of toys, books, or games per child, and line the baskets up side by side, leaving room for each child to spread out. Time them to see how long they take to sort their items into two piles, one to keep and one to donate (and no, they can't keep everything!). Whoever gets done first wins the game.

Since the kids know they are being timed, they don't have time to dwell on whether or not to keep an item; it becomes instinctual. You will be amazed at how quickly your kids are willing to part with items they no longer play with. At the end of the exercise, each child bags up their items to be donated and puts away the items they decided to keep. If you repeat the game two or three times, your kids will declutter and organize their rooms in a matter of minutes!

4) **Give them options.** Many kids, especially as they get older, have trouble parting with things, even if they no longer use them. The good news is that this generation is socially conscious, concerned about the environment, and eager to do service for others. If you take the time to explain where their clothes or toys are going after they leave your house (that is, to children or families in need or perhaps their old preschool), they are more likely to accept, and even embrace, the idea of donating their belongings.

True Story: I was once working with a client's 11-year-old, who refused to part with three garbage bags filled with stuffed animals. When I asked him why, he simply responded, "Because I don't want them to end up in a landfill." When I explained that he could donate some of them to the SPCA for animals in the shelter, he happily donated all but three of his collection! When he realized he had a viable option, he was more than willing to part with them. What's even more important is that he learned he could help others while also helping to organize his own space.

5) **Hold them accountable.** Kids are wonderful at taking things out to play with, but why do so few put things away? It sounds easy enough. Why are so many parents running around picking up after their kids? More often than not, it comes down to one word: convenience. Sure, it's easier for the parent to whip through the room and put everything away, but what message does that send the children? Taking a few extra minutes to show them where everything goes and why it's important benefits everyone in the long run. Being organized isn't just about having a pretty space.

- It teaches respect for one's belongings.
- It provides a sense of responsibility and ownership.
- It instills a sense of pride and gratitude for your home.

I'm not suggesting you should never help your kids; of course there are times when you need to get it done and get out the door quickly. However, when the time comes for them to take the reins, don't you want them to be equipped with the strategies to get the job done? As the mom of two teenagers, I can tell you firsthand that many of my friends wish they didn't enable their kids so much when they were young!

I am a firm believer that being part of a family is a team sport. Everyone plays a role—some larger than others—but every person is important to the overall success of the team. My kids knew from an early age that I don't work for them (that's actually the line I use). As a parent, I will do things for them, but as they grow, I want them to learn life skills—whether it's putting their dishes in the sink, setting the table, or doing their laundry—so they can function on their own.

The more you empower your kids to own part of the process, the more time you will have in your day—not just for you, but also for them. When my kids were small, they wanted to spend time with me after dinner, whether it was playing a game, reading a book, or watching TV. I made it clear that I wanted to spend time with them too, but that the dinner dishes needed to be done first. If they were to help me, we could get it done quicker, leaving more time for us.

What I did was create a value for them to help. They knew that if they participated, they would not only be helping mom, but they would be getting what they wanted—my time.

Tip: If you need more guidance, download a 30-day checklist for organizing with kids for free from my website. The idea came to me as I was looking at my daughter's hoarder-ish room and realized she needed an action plan to get organized.

For many kids, staying on task is often a challenge. A checklist with daily responsibilities can be an effective way to keep them motivated and focused. Each activity is simple, quick, and requires minimal supervision (woohoo!). The challenges range from donating 10 stuffed animals to unloading the dishwasher. The overall goal is to teach three things:

1) Independence

2) Accountability

3) Responsibility

Although you can apply the checklist throughout the year, I loved the idea of implementing it during the summer when kids have more downtime. I geared the tasks to school-age kids, but anyone can participate; simply substitute any task that does not apply with something more appropriate, such as sorting the mail, recycling old magazines, and so on. The point is to have them do something every day to show that a little bit goes a long way. At the end of the month they will have quantifiable proof of their accomplishments.

Responsibility List by Age

Ages 2-3

- ➤ Pick up toys with supervision.
- ➤ Throw things in the trash.
- ➤ Put dirty clothes in the hamper.

Ages 4-6

- ➤ Make their bed with supervision.
- ➤ Get dressed with minimal parental help.
- ➤ Pick up toys with supervision.
- ➤ Wash hands independently.
- ➤ Brush teeth with supervision.
- ➤ Set the table with supervision.
- ➤ Clear their plate from the table.
- ➤ Help a parent prepare food.
- ➤ Assist with sorting clothes for laundry.
- ➤ Help dust.

Ages 7-9

- ➤ Make their bed every day.
- ➤ Choose the day's outfit and get dressed.
- ➤ Maintain general hygiene: Wash hands, brush teeth, comb hair, shower.
- ➤ Pick up toys.
- ➤ Help a parent prepare food.
- ➤ Set the table.
- ➤ Clear their plate from the table.
- ➤ Put away dishes from the dishwasher.
- ➤ Assist with sorting clothes for laundry.
- ➤ Help take care of pet.
- ➤ Fold laundry with supervision.
- ➤ Put laundry in their drawers and closets.
- ➤ Help dust.
- ➤ Empty indoor trash cans.
- ➤ Write thank you notes with supervision.

Ages 10-12

- ➤ Take care of personal hygiene.
- ➤ Keep bedroom clean.
- ➤ Take responsibility for homework.
- ➤ Take responsibility for their belongings.
- ➤ Write thank you notes for gifts.
- ➤ Help wash the family car with supervision.
- ➤ Get their own snack.
- ➤ Clean the bathroom with supervision.
- ➤ Assist with yard work: Rake leaves, pick weeds, help plant and water flowers.
- ➤ Learn to use the washer and dryer.
- ➤ Put laundry away.
- ➤ Help take care of pet.
- ➤ Take the trashcan to the curb for pick up.

Ages 13-15

- ➤ Take care of personal hygiene, belongings, and homework.
- ➤ Write invitations and thank you notes.
- ➤ Wake up and go to bed independently.
- ➤ Maintain personal items, such as charging electronic devices.
- ➤ Keep their rooms clean.
- ➤ Help with all household chores.
- ➤ Mow the lawn independently.
- ➤ Babysit and/or pet sit.
- ➤ Prepare basic meals: Eggs, grilled cheese, soup, and so on.
- ➤ Do assigned housework without prompting.

Ages 16-18

- ➤ Take responsibility for all of the above.
- ➤ Earn spending money.
- ➤ Take care any car they drive.

CHAPTER 19

Reclaiming Time

———

WE'VE TALKED A LOT ABOUT organizing your stuff, but how about finding time in your day for you? Calendar clutter, in my opinion, is the driving force behind so much of our daily stress, anxiety, and frustration. So many of us run on autopilot, especially when the kids are small, or when we are busy taking care of ailing parents or building a career. It's easy to see how we can lose sight of making time for other things in our life that are important, like self-care.

As a society, we have a difficult time knowing how to unplug. Life is filled with distractions, and unless you make a conscious effort to prioritize time for yourself, it will never happen. Maybe you want time to exercise, join a book club, volunteer, or take up a hobby, but figuring out the logistics may seem impossible.

If you're a stay-at-home parent, perhaps you feel riddled with guilt like I used to when my kids were small. I thought, "How dare I leave my babies to do something for myself?"

or "I'm not bringing in a paycheck, so I feel guilty spending money to do something for me."

Reclaiming time for yourself doesn't have to cost a lot. You could take a walk or read a book from the library. The hardest part is prioritizing your needs without feeling guilty (not an easy concept for many of us!).

Whether you make an arrangement with your spouse that every Saturday morning you go to Pilates while he takes the kids, or you set aside 30 minutes before the kids get up each morning to plan your day in quiet, find something that allows you to recharge. Even if it means getting up a little earlier or delegating a task to someone else, if you value your sanity, it's worth it.

Maybe you're in a different boat—trying to build a career and feeling as though you need to say yes to every opportunity that comes your way. I know this pitfall only too well. When I was developing the Simply B Organized brand, I wanted to do anything and everything I could to get clients and build a strong reputation. Ironically, the more I pulled myself in different directions, the less productive I became. I felt as though I was on a never-ending treadmill, always moving but not getting closer to where I wanted to be. It was frustrating and demotivating.

Only when I took a step back to look at what my goals were, and actually wrote down what I had been doing, was I able to see where I needed to change. Note the key phrase: "I needed to change." I had to reclaim control over how I chose to spend my time. Let me give you an example of what I mean:

True story: *When I started Simply B Organized, I would see clients any day of the week. Sometimes I worked six days a week, and other times I worked one. During the weeks I was busy, I was stressed, my house was a mess, I ordered takeout because I didn't have time to shop or cook, and when I finally had a day off, I spent it playing catch up from the prior week. After months of this, I decided to set a schedule of on-site and office days. I even factored in a time to meet friends for lunch or do something for myself (like get my hair done or whatever!).*

I decided Mondays would be office days—to catch up, write my blog, do research for clients, or deal with administrative stuff. This meant I could cook dinner on Monday nights, since I would be working from home all day. If I were feeling ambitious, sometimes I'd even prep Tuesday's dinner! My on-site client days would be Tuesdays, Wednesdays, and Thursdays, and I deemed Wednesdays as takeout night, often letting the girls decide what to order. Thursdays we would also have dinner a home, but since I knew my schedule in advance, I could prepare. Lastly, I dedicated Fridays as my day to run work and personal errands. If I had to go to Target for a client, I would tie it into stuff I needed for the house. While I was out, maybe I'd meet a friend for lunch. As for dinner, we would typically go out or order pizza, so no stress there.

Of course, the key to my new schedule was flexibility. If a client is only able to meet on a Friday, then I would make an exception, but I would try to swap another day for errands so my schedule remained consistent. The point was to establish a routine that I could depend on. At first I was afraid I would lose business by telling people I could only see them on certain days and times, but then I realized that wasn't the case at all. As a matter of fact, my schedule filled up more quickly, and I was able to prioritize my jobs, tasks, and growing business more effectively.

I'm not suggesting it's easy. Starting a career requires discipline, and having small kids at home makes that difficult. Now that my kids are older, it's easier for me to reclaim time. Make no mistake though: I chose to be a martyr for many years. When you never take time for yourself, eventually you get to a point where you feel tired and resentful. This holds true for both home and business.

It's a matter of changing your mindset from feeling guilty to realizing that your physical and emotional wellness are the backbone of your family unit. I'm not suggesting that you jet away every weekend and leave your loved ones to fend for themselves, but carving out 30 to 60 minutes a few times a week is not too much to ask. I have a hunch you would find time in your schedule to help someone else if they needed you.

I ask my clients: "Why are your needs any less important?" Taking time to finish writing this book is a prime example of me reclaiming time. In case you were wondering, it's been five years in the making. I started writing, and then

I stopped. When other things took priority, this got put on a backburner—sometimes for months at a time. I finally got to the point where I said to myself, "If I don't go away for a few days to finish this, it's never going to happen."

Thankfully, my family was in a place where they could function without me, and I went away without guilt. If there is one thing I have learned, it's that life is short, so make time for what matters, including yourself.

"Start where you are. Use what
you have. Do what you can."

—Arthur Ashe

Part 3: Organizing By Space

———

PART 3 IS INTENDED AS a resource guide for organizing specific areas of the home. Feel free to skip around or read them all at once. With each space you organize, you'll still apply the strategies discussed in Part 2 (like using organizational ESP, making four piles, and being mindful of the five clutter pitfalls), but because each area of the home has unique challenges, Part 3 provides some additional things to think about. Apply what works for your particular situation. If six months from now you decide it's time to clean out a particular room, turn to the applicable chapter in Part 3 to get started.

CHAPTER 20

Kitchens

———

WHY THE KITCHEN GETS TO BE A MESS

KITCHENS ARE THE HUB OF the home. That's where many of us spend most of our waking hours. Whether cooking, paying bills, helping with homework, doing arts and crafts projects, or enjoying a glass of wine with friends, the kitchen is always hard at work. Go to any party, and the one room you're bound to find people congregating in is the kitchen. Large or small, it doesn't matter—everyone seems to wind up there. Why? The answer is simple: Kitchens represent comfort, family, friends, and laughter.

The kitchen can also be a source of anxiety and stress— especially if it's not organized efficiently. No matter how organized yours may be, it never seems to stay that way for long. A group of hungry kids can destroy hours of hard work in the blink of an eye, and before you know it, your cabinets can look like a twister hit it. Your kitchen shouldn't look like a museum; it's meant to take a beating. But it doesn't have to look like a tornado ripped through it every time your kids want a snack.

_____

Your Plan of Action

Is there a right or wrong way to organize a kitchen? Of course not. Before you begin, you'll want to consider three things:

* The layout of your space
* Your cooking habits
* Your lifestyle

A common denominator of organizing any kitchen is maximizing space. I've been in countless kitchens that are big and beautiful, but have a poor layout. They lack storage or prep space, proper shelving, or are just too big. On the other hand, some of the most organized and efficient kitchens I've seen have been in small spaces. The difference? Efficient layout. Remember the story I shared in Chapter 14 about the client with a new yet poorly configured kitchen?

Before you apply your organizational ESP and plan a new organizational system for your kitchen, consider five things that are unique to this area of the home:

1) **Define zones**. The first thing to do is begin thinking in terms of the categories you need so you can place

everything logically. Here are some common zones to help you get started:

- Baking
- Cooking
- Spices
- Utensils
- Gadgets
- Pots and pans
- Dry goods
- Dishware
- Glassware
- Dish towels
- Placemats
- Serving dishes
- Office/desk area

2) **Determine Location.** Once you identify the zones you need, figure out the best place for them. To do this, consider:

- Frequency of use
- Volume of goods
- Volume of storage space

3) **Think in terms of prime real estate.** You want to put items with the greatest frequency of use in the most visible and accessible area of the kitchen—your prime real estate. For example if you rarely bake, don't dedicate prime real estate to baking pans.

Instead, use it for items you access more often. On the other hand, if you are an avid baker, dedicating a significant amount of prime storage space to baking supplies may be a good choice.

Consider relocating infrequently used items, like the turkey roaster that only gets used on Thanksgiving, to an overflow area like the garage or basement. That way, you can access it when you need it, but it won't take up valuable real estate.

True story: *One of my favorite stories comes from when I was organizing my friend's kitchen a few years ago. She had a great space above her double ovens that was filled with items she used once a year. On the other hand, there was no proper home for large serving pieces, such as platters and bowls. Considering that my friend does a considerable amount of entertaining throughout the year, it made more sense for her to relocate the infrequently used items to the basement and make better use of her prime real estate.*

4) **Don't limit yourself to kitchen items.** It's okay to think outside the box. As a mother of two kids who both like to do their homework in the kitchen, it made sense for me to dedicate a space to the supplies they used. I repurposed a large kitchen drawer for notebooks, pens, pencils, and other supplies, such as scissors, glue sticks, and erasers. Could I have filled that drawer with a bunch of gadgets I barely use?

Sure. But a better use of the space was to assign it for the kids' supplies. That way, they didn't have to walk to their rooms each time they needed a ruler. Having everything in reach also made for easy cleanup when they were done.

5) **Keep only what you need.** We're all guilty of buying things on impulse that looked cool at the time, but don't work as well as they did on TV. Or perhaps you want to purchase another set of dishes, but your existing dishes are in perfectly good shape; should you keep the old ones? One of the biggest clutter traps in kitchens is duplication. I understand the need for a couple of spatulas, or frying pans of varying sizes, but the items in your kitchen are no different than the clothes in your closet: You use 20% of your stuff 80% of the time.

Here are some tips to help you pare down and organize your kitchen goods:

* Cycle out worn or used items, such as frying pans with scratches, old cutting boards, or worn spatulas.
* Keep no more than two of any given gadget, like measuring spoons and cups or vegetable peelers.
* Check expiration dates for all food—including canned goods, dry goods, and spices—and pitch anything that is past due.

* Some items, like bags of chips, will never sit neatly on a shelf, regardless of how hard you try. Corralling them in bins or baskets is a simple and inexpensive way to make your space appear neat and tidy, even when a fleet of kids comes trampling in after school. Bins are also great for loose items, like granola bars, breads, pasta, and grains, which can get lost on shelving. Pull out the bin to find what you need, and then easily put it back when you're done.

* Keep your spices in an easily accessible place. How many times have you run to the store to buy something you probably own, but can't find? I can't tell you how many times I've come across four bottles of cumin in someone's pantry because it was easier for them to buy a new one rather than tackle the black hole of disorganization. Labeled bins allow you to easily identify what you have so you don't waste time or money on duplicate items.

———

Product Recommendations

* **Tupperware or similar airtight storage containers:** Used to preserve freshness of dry goods, like flour, sugar, pancake mix, and cereal. Also good for leftovers and on-the-go lunches.

- o Why I love them: Easy to label, reusable, versatile, and stackable.
- o Where to get them: Online retailers, Amazon, Bed Bath & Beyond, The Container Store.
- **Open Sterilite Ultra bins**: Great to use in pantries for bagged snacks or lose items. Also good in cabinets to categorize things like spices, flavor packets, or miscellaneous items.
    - o Why I love them: They are versatile, inexpensive, and easy to clean.
    - o Where to get them: Online retailers, Amazon, Target, The Container Store.
- **Drawer dividers:** Ideal for oversized drawers, or drawers that hold multiple categories of items, such as kitchen gadgets or cooking utensils. Also good for junk drawers.
    - o Why I love them: They're customizable (lots of sizes available), inexpensive, and highly functional.
    - o Where to get them: Amazon, Bed Bath & Beyond, Target, The Container Store.

CHAPTER 21

Closets

————

WHY CLOSETS GET TO BE A MESS

WHEN YOUR CONTENTS ARE HIDDEN behind closed doors in closets, it's easy to dismiss what is happening in them. That's why they become "black holes." It's often easier to shut the door and walk away than take time to organize them.

When comments like, "I'll get to it later," or "Just shove it in there for now," become routine, before you know it, your closet looks like a bomb went off inside it. (Think back to procrastination, one of the five clutter pitfalls.)

A lot of emotional clutter lives within our closets as well. Items that cost a lot of money, like those expensive shoes you'll never wear again, or those jeans you may fit into again one day. (FYI, mine were a Lucky Brand, and they looked great, but I could barely get them over my hips now!).

If you can relate, then you know something has got to give. Your closet should be pretty and functional. Most of us need to get dressed quickly and efficiently. There's nothing worse than standing in front of a closet filled with clothes, only to think: "I have nothing to wear."

———

Your Plan of Action

Don't wait for the closet rod to collapse to bite the bullet and go through your clothes! There is no denying it's a time-consuming initiative filled with trying things on, but in the end, you'll be so glad you did.

Before you apply your organizational ESP, consider a few things that are unique to this area of the home:

1) **Reduce volume.** One of the most common reasons closets become disorganized is volume. News flash: You have more clothes than you need. We wear 20% of our clothes 80% of the time. If I looked in your closet, I bet I would find three to five variations of the same thing. Whether it's shoes, tops, or jeans, we all have a look and gravitate toward similar items. That's fine, but what you don't want is to have so much of one thing that you forget what you have, or worse, where you put it. I mean, how many black tank tops can one person own?

2) **Don't be tempted to skip the E in organizational ESP.** If you've ever tried to organize a closet with the contents in it, you will realize that it is next to

impossible. The most effective way to proceed is to empty it and lay everything out. Once you do, there is no turning back, and the empty closet lets you see the space better and determine the best layout for your belongings. Also, having your clothes laid out makes it is easier to sort the things you plan to keep.

3) **You can phone a friend.** If you feel indecisive and need backup, call a friend to help. It never hurts to have moral support along the way! Sometimes having someone else give you permission to purge something is all the incentive you need.

4) **Size Doesn't Matter.** The key to an organized closet is not size, it's maximizing the space to fit your needs. Don't let the size of your closet dictate whether you live with clutter. A large closet isn't synonymous with an organized closet. Some of the most disorganized closets I've seen have been spacious walk-ins. More space only equals more stuff. Likewise, just because you have a small closet doesn't mean you have to live with clutter. Speaking from personal experience, maintaining organization in a small closet requires a higher level of discipline, but it is absolutely possible.

True story: I used to live in a studio apartment with my husband (before children), and although our closet space was very limited, we still managed to keep it organized. To create more space, we reduced the amount of clothes we owned and stored seasonal items under our bed. We also maximized our one not-so-big closet by adding bins below the hanging rod, which doubled our shoe storage.

Assess Your Habits

Now that you've done the hard part, you can breathe a sigh of relief and pat yourself on the back. You are in the home stretch. You have completed your organizational ESP, and hopefully have removed everything except the keep pile from your room. The keep pile contains the only things going back into your closet. For many of you, this may seem shocking since you are so used to looking at a space overflowing with clutter. Remember my earlier statistic: We use 20% of our belongings 80% of the time. It's no wonder your closet may look sparse; you've just purged a majority of goods, but that's okay! You always want to leave room for growth.

Before you begin putting everything back I want you to ask yourself some important questions:

1) **Do I like to fold or hang my clothes?** The answer comes down to personal preference and space. I prefer to hang things. I feel it's a time saver to have everything right in front of you, and I find it easier to shop my closet that way. I also find I rotate my wardrobe more often this way, as opposed to only wearing the shirts on the top of a folded pile. Another bonus is that your clothes don't get as wrinkled when they hang, a great perk for someone like me, who

hates to iron! However many people, especially guys, like their clothes folded. There is no right or wrong choice. The only thing wrong thing would be not finding what you are looking for. If you're unsure of what works, think back to your organizational style. Are you a cognitive or visual person? Would you prefer to see your items out in the open or would you rather everything neatly inside a drawer?

2) **Am I maximizing the space to the best of my ability?** People tend to overlook valuable real estate behind doors, on top of shelves, and in awkward corners of closets. Hooks, bins, and baskets are all inexpensive options to help make use of otherwise wasted space. If you can, add a second hanging rod below your existing one, which actually doubles your hanging real estate. Also, you can hang things inexpensively through the use of a modular hanging rod (available at Bed Bath & Beyond, The Container Store, or Amazon). If you want to completely redo your closet, you can invest in a closet system ranging from a few hundred dollars to several thousand dollars. Regardless of your needs or budget, there are always options! My personal favorites are Organized Living and Elfa because they are moderately priced, offer a variety of options in terms of both color and components, and are adjustable as your needs change. (I am not a paid consultant for either company, just sharing my two cents.)

3) **Are my hangers contributing to my disorganization?** Yes, it's somewhat cosmetic, but if you are investing your valuable time into organizing your closet, why not go the extra mile and invest in matching hangers. Most people have a hodge-podge of assorted hangers in their closet. What you may not realize is that varying hangers by size and shape allows your clothes to sit at varying lengths. Something as simple as investing in the same hangers for all your clothes will have a huge visual impact on the organized appearance of your space. I prefer thin velvet hangers for smaller closets, since the slim design allows you to maximize every inch of the closet rod. If you have a larger walk-in closet, you may want to invest in wooden hangers with notches or flocking at the ends to help make sure your clothes don't slide off. They take up more space on the closet rod, but they are good for heavier items, such as suits or coats.

My goal when organizing any closet is to make it functional and calming. Most of us are not hanging out in our closets. As nice as we want it to be, ultimately we need to be able to find what we need quickly and easily. Who has time to waste stressing out looking for things through piles of clothes on the floor or shoved on a shelf? Not me, and I doubt you do either.

Five things to keep in mind as you organize your closet:

1. Avoid stuffing it to capacity.

2. Invest in matching hangers.

3. Zone your clothes by color and style.

4. Swap your clothes out seasonally if space is an issue.

5. Maximize vertical space.

———

PRODUCT RECOMMENDATIONS

*   **Huggable velvet hangers:** Maximize space and ensure your clothes sit at the same height with slim velvet hangers.
    *   Why I love them: Inexpensive, space-saving, aesthetically pleasing.
    *   Where to get them: Amazon, Target, The Container Store, HomeGoods, HSN.
*   **Wooden hangers:** Great for men's suits and heavy outwear, or if you have a large luxury closet and are willing to invest in quality hangers.

- o Why I love them: They can withstand the weight of heavy items, like coats and suits, and are aesthetically pleasing.
- o Where to get them: Online retailers like Amazon, Home Depot, Lowe's, Target, The Container Store.

- **Bins and baskets:** Ideal for underwear, workout clothes, purses, and anything in between.
  - o Why I love them: They keep clutter at bay, making it easy for you to quickly find what you need.
  - o Where to get them: Online retailers like Amazon, Pottery Barn, Target, Wayfair, HomeGoods, The Container Store.

- **Clear shoe bins:** Great space saver for storing multiple pairs of shoes in a small space.
  - o Why I love them: You can purchase them by the case fairly inexpensively. They are versatile and can be used for other things aside from shoes, like purses, scarves, and wallets.
  - o Where to get them: Online retailers like Amazon, Bed Bath & Beyond, Target, The Container Store.

- **Valet hooks:** These are great for pulling out your clothes the night before.
  - o Why I love them: They don't take up much room, but provide additional hanging space for prepping outfits.
  - o Where to get them: Typically purchased with your closet system.

- **Belt and tie racks:** Depending on your volume and space, you can choose from wall-mounted, rotating racks or hanging solutions for belts and ties. Whichever you choose, just make sure you can access what you need without a lot of fuss.
  - Why I love them: Having one designated spot to go to for belts or ties makes getting ready a snap.
  - Where to get them: Online retailers like Amazon, Bed, Bath, & Beyond, Target, HomeGoods, The Container Store.
- **Hooks inside closet doors:** If you have a hinged door, I recommend placing hanging hooks on the inside for hoodies, robes, and other items that can be hung.
  - Why I love them: Hooks are an inexpensive way to add real estate to an otherwise wasted space. It's nice to have a "drop spot" for quick grab-and-go items. In our house, we all have hooks inside our closet doors; I use mine to hang dry cleaning, the girls use theirs to hang sweatshirts. Whatever you choose, it's a convenient and clutter-free solution!
  - Where to get them: Online retailers like Amazon, Home Depot, Lowe's, Target, The Container Store.
- **Hamper and/or dry cleaning bin:** Depending on space, you may want to consider having a hamper

and/or dry cleaning bin inside your closet to make getting undressed easier.

- o   Why I love them: Having a hamper and dry cleaning bin close by leaves no excuse for clothes to end up on the floor!
- o   Where to get them: Online retailers like Amazon, Bed Bath & Beyond, Target, HomeGoods, The Container Store.

CHAPTER 22

Bathrooms

WHY BATHROOMS GET TO BE A MESS

TUBES OF TOOTHPASTE, MAKEUP, LOTIONS, and medicine are just a few culprits that add to bathroom chaos. Random items get sucked into the black hole of under-sink cabinets, never to be heard from again. Add the chaos of trying to get ready in a timely fashion for school or work, and you quickly realize that having an organized bathroom is more important than you would think.

YOUR PLAN OF ACTION

Here's some good news: Bathrooms are one of the easiest rooms to organize. There's no paper clutter, minimal emotional clutter, and lots of goodies with expiration dates to take the guesswork out of purging.

Before you apply your organizational ESP and plan a new organizational system for your bathroom, consider a few things that are unique to this area of the home:

1) **Less is more**. Bathrooms typically have lots of little things that can quickly get out of control if not nipped in the bud. The best thing you can do is to streamline what you have. When it comes to bathrooms, less is more! If you buy in bulk, it doesn't mean you need to store 24 rolls of toilet paper under your sink. Keep a few rolls on hand, and let the rest live in your overflow storage area. If you don't have one, I recommend buying smaller quantities.

2) **Define zones.** Begin by identifying what categories apply to your things. Once you have them identified, sort your goods and define the zones you will place them in, keeping like with like. Below are a few category ideas to consider:
   - **Hygiene**: Soap, deodorant, razors, Q-tips
   - **Oral care**: Toothbrushes, toothpaste, dental floss, mouthwash
   - **Hair care**: Shampoo, conditioner, styling products, hair accessories, brushes, combs, blow dryer, curling iron, straightening iron
   - **First-aid**: Band-Aids, peroxide, rubbing alcohol, ointments, creams
   - **Sun care**: Sunscreen, aloe
   - **Medicine**: Pain relievers and other over-the-counter medications

* **Paper products**: Toilet paper, tissues, feminine hygiene products
* **Travel**: I recommend keeping travel-size toiletries in a lidded bin for business trips, vacations, or sleepovers. You only need a few of each category, so no need to swipe the hotel shampoo every time you go away!

3) **Sheets and towels.** If you keep sheets in a bathroom closet, consider this rule of thumb: You only need one extra set of sheets per bed, plus a set of flannel sheets. Purge any mismatched sets. If you have frequent out-of-town guests, you can add one additional set for each guest bed. As for towels, assign three to four sets of towels per person. If you wash your face with washcloths everyday, I recommend having a set of eight in case you only wash your towels once a week.

4) **Keep things separate.** Here are some ways to keep the things you keep in your bathroom from comingling:
* **Linen closets:** If you are fortunate enough to have a linen closet, use it wisely! Place a wall-mounted or over-the-door storage unit on the inside of the door for things like first-aid, sunscreen, hygiene, and oral care.

* **Sheets:** If you are not an expert folder (I am not!), use this little trick: Get same-size baskets and label each one by size or by person (e.g., "full size sheets" or "Johnny's sheets"). Fold each set of sheets and store it in the corresponding bin. This way, when you need to change sheets you don't have to go hunting through piles of linens to find the right size. Opening a closet to find a shelf of neatly organized bins is a lot more refreshing than praying nothing topples on you as you open the door!

* **Vanity:** If your bathroom vanity has drawers, I recommend getting drawer dividers or organizers to maintain order. Otherwise, investing in some stand-alone storage solutions, such as a rolling cart, to hold your stuff is the way to go. Use small bins or baskets for loose items to reduce visual clutter.

* **Under-sink storage:** Most under-sink storage is a breeding ground for clutter. Typically there is about two feet of vast space with a drainpipe in the middle. Any time you can add pullout shelving to a cabinet, you automatically increase the amount of functional space, since items tend to get lost in the back. There are several inexpensive options that require little to no assembly and can double your usable space.

* **Hooks:** Many items can be hung in a bathroom, like robes, towels, and washcloths. People tend to overlook prime real estate behind doors or next to

the tub, where you can maximize otherwise wasted space. Think in terms of accessibility: If you have little kids, hang hooks within their reach. It's never too early to foster good organizing habits.

———

PRODUCT RECOMMENDATIONS:

- **Stacked, under-sink, pullout storage units:** Great for cleaning supplies, toilet paper, hair products, and assorted overflow items.
  - o Why I love them: They make use of the wasted space often found in vanities. Pullouts in any space allow you to maximize the depth of your cabinet so items in the back don't get lost or forgotten.
  - o Where to get them: Online retailers like Amazon, Bed Bath & Beyond, Target, Home Depot, Lowe's, The Container Store.
- **Drawer dividers:** If you have a vanity with drawers, dividers are a great way to store things like tweezers, makeup, or hair supplies that are often shoved randomly in places.
  - o Why I love them: It makes things easy to find. Who wants to search for a bobby pin when trying to put their hair up?

- o Where to get them: Online retailers like Amazon, Bed Bath & Beyond, Target, HomeGoods, The Container Store.
- **Baskets for sheets:** Great for organizing and storing sheets in the way I describe above.
  - o Why I love them: They are worth it for the sheer convenience of opening up the closet and knowing what to grab. Plus, no more stressing about perfectly folding those awful fitted sheets!
  - o Where to get them: Online retailers like Amazon, Bed Bath & Beyond, Target, HomeGoods, Pottery Barn, Wayfair, The Container Store.
- **Wall-mounted storage units:** Anywhere you can use a wall or door for storage is a bonus in my book! Depending on the size and shape of your bathroom, you can find some unique products at random places, like flea markets or antique stores.
  - o Why I love them: Not everyone has a linen closet in his or her bathroom, so wall-mounted storage is another inexpensive way to add real estate to a small space.
  - o Where to get them: Online retailers like Amazon, Bed Bath & Beyond, Target, HomeGoods, The Container Store.
- **Hampers:** Some people prefer to keep their hampers in their bathrooms because they get undressed right before hopping in the shower or tub. A hamper doesn't have to be fancy. I use a laundry basket in the bottom of my girls' linen closet for their dirty duds!

o   Why I love them: Using a laundry basket as a hamper skips a step: It saves time transferring dirty clothes from the hamper to the laundry basket. It also allows me to take advantage of the space in their bathroom. Most hampers are tall and narrow, but by using a laundry basket, I only sacrifice low shelf space. Another bonus is that they know, when the basket is full, it's time to throw in a load of wash!

o   Where to get them: Online retailers like Amazon, Bed Bath & Beyond, Target, HomeGoods, The Container Store.

CHAPTER 23

Playrooms

WHY PLAYROOMS GET TO BE A MESS

BY DEFINITION, PLAYROOMS ARE DESIGNED to be spaces where kids make a mess. The goal with organizing a playroom is to create an inviting space that is not overwhelming. Kids are no different than adults; they play with 20% of their toys 80% of the time, which goes to show that, like us, they have too much stuff. In this chapter, I address common playroom pitfalls and how to avoid them.

YOUR PLAN OF ACTION

There is no escaping the fact that playrooms require frequent maintenance. Kids should have a safe place to be creative, have fun, and make a mess. Equally important is teaching your children the importance of valuing their items and cleaning up when they finish playing.

I speak with countless parents who don't dare step foot in the playroom for fear of being instantly overwhelmed. If the sight of toys all over the floor stresses you out, what makes you think your child won't feel the same? Earlier, we established that clutter causes stress. That anxiety doesn't differentiate between children and adults. Chances are if a messy room stresses you out, it is stressing your kids out, too.

Knowing where to begin is the hardest part. Before you apply your organizational ESP and plan a new organizational system for your playroom, consider a few things that are unique to this area of the home:

1) **Assess your space.** It's amazing how quickly an empty room can get filled up with kids' toys, games, crafts, puzzles, dolls, action figures ... I could go on, but you get the general idea. Whether your playroom is a space unto itself, or a corner of your family room, think about what's not working and what you want to improve. Define where you want toys to live, and how you can prevent overflow into non-toy zones. Also, think about ways to maximize the space by finding solutions that pull double-duty, like window seats with storage, art tables with shelving, and ottomans with storage.

2) **Gauge your inventory.** Inventory is by far the biggest complaint parents make about trying to keep an organized play space: "My kids have too many toys!"

Kids tend to play with the same toys day in and day out. The rest may only to see the light of day when company comes over. In addition to applying your organizational ESP, try temporarily removing items your kids don't use, then seeing if they miss them. If they don't ask for them back, consider donating or cycling them in rotation at a later time. For more tips, see Chapter 18: Getting the Kids Involved.

3) **Create an inviting layout.** Once you've assessed the space and inventory, it's time to create an inviting new layout. Playrooms should function no differently than any other space in your home. Creating defined zones is a simple and effective way to stay organized. For example, you can create a reading corner, or what I like to call a book nook, where kids can grab a book and sit quietly away from distractions. When my girls were young, we had a pretend-play zone, which had a puppet theater, a bin of puppets, and a plethora of dress-up clothes. It was great for them to be able to move from space to space without feeling overwhelmed. Defining zones also simplifies cleanup, since everyone knows exactly where everything belongs.

Tip: If you can incorporate natural light into the room, do it. Kids love to look out windows, and adding seating near them is a great way to bring the outdoors inside.

4) **Establish a system for easy access and cleanup.** I believe in fostering independence and accountability in children. Whenever I am asked to help design a playroom, I am cognizant of making sure that items are well within the reach of a child. Obviously, there are certain items, like paints and Playdoh, which you may want your child to use under supervision, so keeping those items out of reach is a good idea. However, they should be able to access the majority of toys—like cars, LEGOS, Barbies, puzzles, and books—on their own. Using colorful bins and baskets to corral like items makes cleanup easier and faster for kids, but keep it simple. If you ask your kids to color-code their LEGOS, you're making more work for everyone. The goal of these is to get them into the habit of cleaning up after themselves.

Tip: Label bins with pictures rather than words if your child is too young to read.

5) **Periodically purge.** Once you set up your new playroom system, be prepared to purge periodically. This is often the most stressful part of the process, and sometimes it's the parents that stress out more than the kids! That said, it's crucial to keeping the system organized. I don't believe in purging while the kids are asleep. Have I ever tossed a broken toy without consulting my child? Absolutely. However, the only way your kids will learn how to organize

is to do it with you. People often ask me how often to purge a playroom, but there is no right answer. It depends on the ages of the kids, how often new toys come into rotation, and how often they play with what's in front of them. To stay ahead of the clutter, most playrooms should have a big purge at least twice a year: Once just before the winter holidays (to make room for new toys, as well as to get rid of unused or broken toys), and once right after school gets out (to adapt to the kids' transition from one grade to the next). Establishing a purging schedule allows you to make small tweaks along the way, reducing the overwhelming feeling of bigger purges for you and your kids.

Tip: Use the opportunity to teach a life lesson. Teaching your kids the value in donating items they no longer play with to those who are less fortunate is something they will carry with them into adulthood.

———

Product Recommendations

* **Open bins and baskets**: Good for easy sorting and cleanup of toys. Be careful that you don't get really deep bins and baskets, which can quickly become black holes.

o   Why I love them: They have style and allow you to get creative without spending a fortune.

o   Where to get them: Online retailers like Amazon, Target, HomeGoods, The Container Store.

- **Clear-lidded shoebox bins:** Great for art supplies that you want to keep out of the reach of small children.

o   Why I love them: Clear lidded bins are so inexpensive, yet so functional. They stack easily and allow you to quickly see the contents without having to open the lid.

o   Where to get them: Online retailers like Amazon, Bed Bath & Beyond, Target, The Container Store.

- **Seating areas:** Depending on the size of your space, it's always nice to incorporate different places for kids and parents to sit, whether it's a window seat, a comfy chair, or a set of beanbag chairs.

o   Why I love them: Even though most kids enjoy playing on the floor, it's nice to have a spot to sit and read a book. When my older daughter was a baby, we turned a corner of our guest room into a reading nook for her, and although it wasn't a large space, every night after her bath she picked out a book and we sat together there to read a story.

o   Where to get them: You can find some great kid chairs at Pottery Barn, Amazon, Wayfair, Ikea, and Target.

* **A table and chairs:** Like seating areas, this isn't a must-have, but it's nice if you have the space. A kid-height table and chairs can be used for coloring projects, art projects, puzzles, or games. If you are going to invest in one, I strongly suggest you get one with built-in storage.
  o Why I love them: It's nice to have a place other than your kitchen table for the kids to work and play, plus the added storage allows you to free up space for other items.
  o Where to get them: Online retailers like Amazon, Pottery Barn, Ikea, Land of Nod, Target, Wayfair.
* **Bookshelves:** Kids love books, and even before they know how to read, they like to look at the pictures. Make sure that books are easily accessibility for young kids, especially if you have climbers!
  o Why I love them: Reading is important for kids' growth and development. Allowing them to explore books that interest them is a wonderful learning tool.
  o Where to get them: Online retailers like Amazon, Pottery Barn, Ikea, Land of Nod, Target, Wayfair.
* **Area rugs:** Kids like to play on the floor. They sit, crawl, and even roll around. If you have hardwood floors, it can get cold for little feet.
  o Why I love them: Area rugs tie a room together without costing a fortune. They can reflect your

style and act as a divider if the playroom shares space with another part of the house.
- o Where to get them: Online retailers like Amazon, HomeGoods, Home Decorator Collection, Ikea, Land of Nod, Target, Wayfair.
- ❀ **Good lighting sources:** Don't underestimate the importance of good lighting, especially if your playroom is in the basement or a back bedroom. I shy away from floor lamps because they're easily knocked over. If possible, opt for recessed ceiling lights that are safe from swinging light sabers or swords!
  - o Why I love them: Good lighting can brighten any space and help keep little eyes focused!
  - o Where to get them: Online retailers like Amazon, Home Depot, Lowe's.

CHAPTER 24

Dining Rooms

WHY DINING ROOMS GET TO BE A MESS

ONCE UPON A TIME, PEOPLE used formal dining rooms on a regular basis to eat large family meals and host dinner parties. Fast-forward to today, and most people will tell you they use their formal dining room a few times a year at best. So what happens in this room the rest of the year? For many, the dining room table is the natural dumping ground for anything and everything. Other people, like myself, have repurposed the formal dining room for something else.

YOUR PLAN OF ACTION

Many of us treat the dining room as a dumping ground for mail, school projects, and random items we have yet to put away. Since it doesn't get used often, there is no urgency to organize the space, and it's easy for clutter to collect.

If clutter in your dining room is stressing you out, use the five W's:

- **Who** is the main offender? You? Your spouse? The kids?
- **What** type of clutter is filling up the table? Mail? Bills? Presents to be wrapped?
- **Where** should those items live? Do they have a proper home?
- **When** do I use this room? To pay bills? Work on projects? As a holding place for things I have to I get to?
- **Why** do I allow the dining room to act as a clutter catchall? Am I too busy? Unsure of where the items should live? Out of convenience?

If you opt to keep the space as intended, but want to keep it clutter-free, you'll need to designate a proper home for the items that have been taking up residence on your dining room table.

Tip: Set the table. If you stage your dining room as if you were having a dinner party, it prohibits you from using the table as a dumping ground, plus it creates a warm and inviting feeling for the space.

––––

PRODUCT RECOMMENDATIONS

There is no law that states your formal dining room has to stay as intended. I have seen people convert this formal space into something more functional. Here are a few options if you are thinking along these lines:

- **A playroom:** The dining room is typically located directly off the kitchen, which makes it a great space for the kids' toys. That way, the little ones can play within earshot, while parents cook dinner in the next room or help older siblings with homework.
    - o Why I love it: Kids like to be close to their parents when they are young. Even though we had a beautifully finished basement for my kids to play in when they were toddlers, they only wanted to be down there if I joined them. Not the most ideal situation when you are trying to make dinner! Converting the dining room to a play space provides your kids with the security of having you close by, but allows you to do other things.
- **An office:** If you don't have a dedicated workspace, want a space for the kids to do their homework, or need a home for shared computers, converting a formal dining room into an office might be a great option.
    - o Why I love it: Most dining rooms have a ceiling fixture, so you don't have to worry about poor lighting. And since they are usually off the kitchen, it's a good location for multi-tasking.
- **A music room or sitting room:** Many people play instruments, but don't have a great practice space and

end up rehearsing in a bedroom. A converted dining room can be a great space to play guitar (think about mounting them on the wall), play piano, or if you don't play, to sit and relax with a good book.

○   Why I love this: This is exactly what we did in our home several years ago, and we use the space so much more now. Unfortunately, I don't play an instrument, but one of my daughters does. This is where we keep our piano, my daughter's guitars, and a couple of comfy chairs. I call it the keeping room, and often go there to chat with a girlfriend, enjoy a glass of wine, or read a book.

CHAPTER 25

Bedrooms

WHY BEDROOMS GET TO BE A MESS

BEDROOMS ARE EASY CLUTTER TRAPS because you're the only person that sees them. Typically, when guests come over, they don't hang out in your bedroom. Laundry, books, stuffed animals, and knickknacks can quickly take over floor and surface spaces, making the walls feel as though they are closing in around you.

YOUR PLAN OF ACTION

How you think about the organizational challenge of a bedroom depends on whose it is, so this chapter is organized by that principle. Feel free to read all of the bedroom sections, or just the ones that apply to you now.

1) **The master bedroom.** We wake up with the day ahead of us, then go to sleep exhausted. Is clutter

the first thing you see in the morning and the last thing you see at night? If you answered yes, then read on. Your bedroom is supposed to be a place of calm—a retreat after a long day of work or dealing with the kids. Surrounding yourself with clutter is unhealthy both mentally and physically. The good news is that, of all the rooms in the house to keep organized, bedrooms should be fairly simple. They don't get as much traffic as other areas, and usually become disorganized as a result of unmade beds and laundry. Here are some habits you can cultivate to get the master bedroom in order.

- **First things first ... make your bed.** One of the most important lessons my mother taught me was to make my bed when I get up. I'm amazed at how many people skip this important step. Making your bed sets the tone of your room. It implies tidiness rather than disorganization, and makes the room look visually appealing. There have been studies to prove the value of starting and ending your day with a made bed. Even if no one other than you enters the space, and you enter only to crawl back into bed, it's still the first step to an organized bedroom.
- **Put away the laundry.** I dread putting laundry away. Doing laundry is one thing, but folding it and putting it away is another story. Thankfully my husband puts most of our clothes away before I get the chance. That being said, I understand how

tempting it is for people to shop the laundry basket for clean clothes, rather than put laundry away. However, like making your bed, the benefits of walking into a room where everything is in its place outweigh the 10 minutes it takes to do this. Find a distraction to make the task more tolerable. Talk on the phone, listen to music, turn on the TV—whatever it takes to power through the task at hand.

- **Use a hamper.** Instead of leaving the clothes you take off in a heap on the floor, pick them up and put them in a hamper to be washed. It's as simple as that. The reward for retraining yourself is an uncluttered room.

- **Sitting room**. The sitting room that comes with many master bedrooms can be a blessing or a curse. Ideally, it should be a place to quietly read, exercise, scrapbook, or work. However, for most people, it becomes a dumping ground. My best advice is to make it functional. Clutter accumulates when a space is undefined. If you create an area that has a clear purpose, it's easier to keep clutter at bay. One of my clients recently turned her sitting room into a yoga studio. How many times do you long for a Zen space, free from distraction? All she did was remove the furniture, replace the carpet with flooring, add a few inviting accents, and voila!

---

2) **Kids' bedrooms**. The main difference between organizing children's bedrooms and adult bedrooms is that kids' rooms often double as play areas or homework spaces. Like adults, children still need to make their beds, put away their laundry, and keep their clothes off the floor, but when I talk to people, it's clear that the biggest challenge with kids' rooms is finding space for everything!

 - **Create zones:** Regardless of how large or small your child's room is, creating defined zones will help to keep the space organized. Most kids would love to have a space, other than their bed, to entertain friends, so factor in a seating area, if possible. Also having room for kids to play on the floor is important, especially for younger kids, so place furniture around the perimeter of the room, leaving the center open to sit and play.

 - **Make it transient:** As kids grow and mature, their interests change. When you set up this space, you want to make sure it can grow with your child. No one wants their 12 year old stuck in a toddler room.

 - **Workspace.** Some kids prefer to do their homework in their bedroom, so having a designated workspace can be important. However, a desk can be a natural clutter trap and isn't a must. Before you invest money and dedicate prime real estate to one, make sure your child is the type of kid to use it.

❀ **Memory boxes and ledge shelves:** Oh the participation award ... whoever came up with the bright idea to give kids prizes for showing up clearly wasn't concerned about accumulating clutter! Get your child a memory box to collect ribbons and paper awards. They can keep it in the closet and take it out to look at it. Install ledge shelving on walls to display trophies and photos. This keeps dresser tops clear while still showcasing a child's accomplishments (win-win!). They are also great for small, breakable items, like snow globes and other tchotchkes.

———

3) **Guestrooms.** The guestroom has a lot of potential. It can double as an office. It can be used to store presents and wrapping paper. And the closets in this room can be used to house overflow clothes. Let's face it—the possibilities for guestrooms are endless!

❀ **Create zones:** Once you identify how you want or need a guest bedroom to function, it's simply a matter of coming up with a plan of action to get you there. As usual, it's all about defining the space with zones.

- **Use your organizational ESP:** If your guest room is overrun with random clutter, use the process defined in Part 2 of this book to get rid of it. It's okay to use your guest room for overflow items, as long as you're not holding onto things simply because you have the space to do so.
- **Create a sensible layout:** Once the clutter is gone, and you have an idea of what you want to use the space for (i.e.: a craft/wrapping room, sewing room, general hobby room), you can begin to design a layout to maximize the space.

Tip: Incorporate the closet as part of your design. If you do not need to use your guest closet for clothes, consider taking off the doors and incorporating the extra square footage into the room. I've seen closets transformed into craft stations, reading nooks, and workspaces, while a full or queen-size bed remains in the space for out-of-town guests.

———

PRODUCT RECOMMENDATIONS

- **Memory Boxes:** I recommend keeping a small memory box in each person's bedroom for keepsakes, such as cards, letters, or ticket stubs.

- o Why I love them: They allow you to keep miscellaneous items organized and to keep dresser and desktops clutter-free.
- o Where to get them: Online retailers like Amazon, The Container Store, Michaels, HomeGoods.
- **Shelves:** Great for storing trophies, snow globes, tchotchkes, books, or pictures.
  - o Why I love them: There is typically not a lot of counter space in a bedroom, other than a dresser, nightstand, or end table, which fill up quickly. Shelves are a great way to still keep memories visible without being in the way.
  - o Where to get them: Online retailers like Amazon, Home Depot, Target.
- **Hampers:** If you get undressed in your bedroom, or if your bathroom isn't big enough for a hamper, the bedroom is the ideal place for one.
  - o Why I love them: You can fit a hamper almost anywhere—inside a closet, in the corner, even mounted over a door!
  - o Where to get them: Online retailers like Amazon, The Container Store, Bed Bath & Beyond, HomeGoods.
- **Storage bins and baskets:** Ideal for kids' toys if they have space in their room. You can also have a basket with blankets or stuffed animals.
  - o Why I love them: Using a bin or basket to corral things makes the room less cluttered and easier

to clean. It also makes it easy for kids to transport their things from one room to another, the way kids do!

    o   Where to get them: Online retailers like Amazon, Pottery Barn, Land of Nod, Wayfair, Target, HomeGoods.

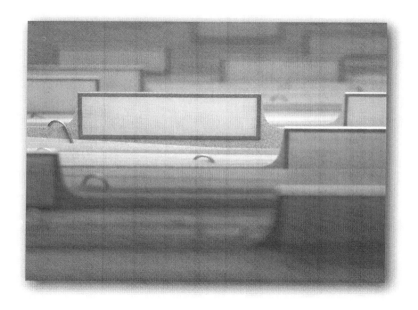

CHAPTER 26

Home Offices

———

WHY A HOME OFFICE GETS TO BE A MESS

ONE WORD: PAPER. WHETHER YOU work full-time out of your home office, or use it to run your household, paper is the leading cause of office disorganization.

Shockingly, the amount of paper we accumulate is actually on the increase! When we don't know what to do with something, our first instinct is to do nothing (remember indecision—one of the five clutter pitfalls?). Usually, we fear making a mistake and not being able to retrieve a lost document.

The reality is that 80% of the papers we file never get looked at again, which means we are keeping more than we need. If you're unsure of what you need to hold onto, flip back to Chapter 5, which includes a cheat sheet for how long you need to keep critical documents.

———

Your Plan of Action

Before you apply your organizational ESP and plan a new organizational system for your office, consider a few things that are unique to this area of the home:

1) **Separate work from home.** If you work from home, keep your work files separate from your personal files. It makes retrieval much easier. I recommend having separate filing systems and inboxes to keep papers from comingling.

2) **Separate action and reference items.** An action item requires you to do something. Examples: A bill that you need to pay, an invitation that needs a response. A reference item is something that you want to keep, but requires no action, other than to be filed. Examples: insurance documents, annual statements. By sorting into piles first, you save time in the long run and also reduce the risk of having something important fall through the cracks.

3) **Store papers vertically.** Storing papers in a manner that allows you to quickly find them (as opposed to rummaging through stacks of papers) saves you valuable time and energy.

4) **Label files for easy retrieval.** One of my clients recently shared a story with me. She needed to find her child's latest health records from the

pediatrician, and within minutes, she had the document in hand, thanks to the easy system we established. Labeling your files will save hours of searching later on.

5) **Create an electronic filing system.** One of the easiest ways to reduce paper clutter is to transition to electronic bills. Doing this saves space, but there's an added bonus, too: Finding an electronic document takes a fraction of the time it takes to sort through stacks of papers.

6) **Make it accessible.** If your home office sits apart from your living area—say, upstairs or above a garage—consider creating a designated command center for incoming mail and papers in your home. Since we are all so busy, it's unrealistic to expect that you are going to run to your home office every time you get a new piece of mail. A command center eliminates the urge to create piles throughout the house.

7) **Create a routine for follow though.** Without execution, the greatest plans are destined to fail unless we commit to follow through. Consistency can be the difference between clutter and calm. If you procrastinate and don't stay a step ahead of paperwork, things are going to fall through the cracks (bills will be late, you'll forget that RSVP, or you'll send your

kid to school without a permission slip). Instead, get in a routine of going though your paperwork daily or weekly.

———

Product Recommendations

- **Command center systems:** Regardless of whether you have a designated home office or use a corner of your kitchen, everyone needs a command center to sort the mail and store action items and papers. It can be a system of baskets and trays that sit on a desk or something mounted on a wall. If you have room, I am a big fan of <u>Pottery Barn's Daily System.</u>
    - o Why I love them: You can customize components to fit your space and meet your needs. Whether you prefer a pin board, corkboard, whiteboard calendar, or letterbox, components are easy to install, and you can switch them out as necessary.
    - o Where to get them: Online retailers like Amazon, Pottery Barn, HomeGoods.
- **Drawer dividers:** A must-have for keeping office supplies organized.
    - o Why I love them: They keep everything in their places—no more searching for paperclips or stamps! Choose options based on the dimensions of your drawers and what you keep on hand.

- ○ Where to get them: Online retailers like Amazon, Staples, Target.
- ❀ **Filing cabinets:** Even though I recommend going digital whenever possible, and shredding or recycling unnecessary paper, there are going to be documents you need to keep. Whether they are insurance papers, medical records, or tax documents, having a good filing system is critical if you ever need to retrieve your information.
  - ○ Why I love them: The good news is that ugly, industrial, metal filing cabinets are a thing of the past. Many filing cabinets now double as furniture. Even if you don't have a designated office, you can organize your papers with style!
  - ○ Where to get them: Target, Ballard Designs, Pottery Barn.
- ❀ **Safes:** If you don't use a safe deposit box, critical documents, such as birth certificates, marriage records, passports, deeds, and wills, should be stored somewhere safe from damage or theft.
  - ○ Why I love them: You know that irreplaceable items are secure. You decide who gets the code and where to store it. Many safes are made to fit under a desk or inside a closet, so they take up less real estate.
  - ○ Where to get them: Online retailers like Amazon or Staples.

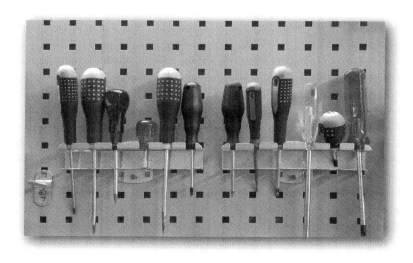

CHAPTER 27

Basements, Garages, Attics, & Sheds

WHY BASEMENTS, GARAGES, ATTICS, & SHEDS GET TO BE A MESS

I OFTEN REFER TO GARAGES, basements, attics, and sheds as the black holes of the home. Things get sucked in, but good luck trying to get them out! Once upon a time, people used to actually park cars in the garage, but today fewer than 20% of all people in the United States actually do this. The majority of people use their garages to store anything and everything from tools, to toys, to seasonal items.

One issue with each of these areas is size. Typically, these rooms are vast open spaces without defined areas for storage or placement of items, making them easy dumping grounds. When thinking about these spaces in terms of the five clutter pitfalls (Chapter 8), many people check all of the boxes: procrastination, indecision, guilt, feeling overwhelmed, and time.

Another common reason that clutter accumulates in these places is we neglect them. We can justify spending money to update a kitchen, bedroom, or bathroom, but for some reason, we get hung up on investing time and money into a basement, garage, or attic.

The good news is that it doesn't have to cost a fortune to organize these spaces, but it does require time (yours or someone else's) to get it decluttered and to get some products installed. However, once you set up a system, these areas are usually easy to maintain.

––––

Your Plan of Action

Before you apply your organizational ESP and plan a new organizational system for your basement, garage, or attic, consider a few things that are unique to these areas of the home:

1) **Understand your needs.** The first thing you'll want to do is figure out what exactly you need from each space. Here are a few questions to ask yourself:
   The basement:
   * Is it finished or unfinished?
   * Is it a playroom?
   * Do you have a laundry area?
   * Are you storing out-of-season clothes?
   * Seasonal items?

- Memorabilia storage?
- Do you avoid going down there because it's a dingy, disorganized mess?

The garage:
- Do you need to store tools?
- Garden supplies?
- Sports equipment?
- Bins of seasonal items?
- Cars?
- Bikes?

The attic:
- Is it easy to access?
- Is it functional to store things (in other words, does it have flooring, lighting, ventilation)?
- If you were to use it for storage, what types of things would you want to keep up there?

The shed:
- What am I storing?
- Gardening tools?
- Snow removal equipment?
- Do I have ample wall space to make use of vertical space?
- Can my shed accommodate shelving to get contents off the floor?

2) **Zone it:** Once you identify what you need from each space, as well as why the space is disorganized,

you can map out the zones that will allow you to do this. Try to keep it simple by making zones somewhat general (for example, sports, gardening, seasonal, automotive). This should make it easier to find what you need quickly. Putting things away is more doable too when you're not hung up on being super specific.

3) **Store UP, not OUT:** Another commonality among these three areas is that most people use them to store oversized items and large storage bins. Think about going vertical and using more wall space than floor space to do this. The key is getting as much off the floor as possible, while still keeping things accessible.

4) **Shelving:** Inexpensive floor-to-ceiling shelving is a great option for unfinished basements, attics, and garages. If your garage ceiling is high enough, you can also have a loft installed for items you only need to access once or twice a year.

5) **Out of sight, out of mind:** If you can, I recommend storing things in clear bins. Even if you plan on labeling, it's so much easier to assess what's inside if you can see the contents.

———

Product Recommendations

* **Wall-mounted systems organizational systems:** Great option for garage storage. There are two I especially like. The components of the Organized Living Freedom Rail all mount on the wall so nothing is on floor, and you can use their online design tool to customize your garage. I have this in my own garage and I love it! The Rubbermaid FastTrack System is another great option for the DIYer looking for an inexpensive, functional solution. This was the first garage system I used and I still recommend it today. It's so simple to install anyone can do it!
  * Why I love them: These solutions provide the look of a high-end custom garage without costing a fortune. The systems offer a variety of interchangeable components to choose from, including stuff for sports, gardening, bikes, open shelving, and closed cabinetry.
  * Where to get them: Online retailers like Amazon, organizedliving.com, Home Depot, Lowes.
* **Loft systems:** If you have high ceilings in your garage, a great option is to install a loft that mounts to the ceiling. I'll be honest in telling you that I don't have one specific brand that I use, but I have purchased several for clients and never had an issue.

- o Why I love them: They are great for storing over-sized bins or things you use infrequently, take up a lot of room, and don't sit nicely on a shelf (like skis or camping equipment). Most lofts are relatively inexpensive (a couple hundred dollars at most) and well worth the investment.
- o Where to get them: Online retailers like Amazon, Home Depot, Wayfair Lowe's.

- **Sterilite clear latched bins:** These are one of my go-to products for storing seasonal items, memorabilia, and decorations.
  - o Why I love them: They are available in a variety of sizes, they are inexpensive, and most importantly, they keep your items safely protected in an airtight container.
  - o Where to get them: Online retailers like Amazon, Home Depot, Lowe's.

- **Stand-alone shelving units:** Shelves can turn garages, attics, or unfinished basements into highly functional spaces. My favorite brands are Edsel, Husky, and Sterilite, depending on what I am storing and how much room I have available.
  - o Why I love them: This type of shelving is great for everything from paint cans, to overflow pantry items, or seasonal bins.
  - o Where to get them: Home Depot and Lowe's have a host of options that will suit the size of your space.

CHAPTER 28

Mudrooms & Laundry Rooms

————

WHY MUDROOMS AND LAUNDRY ROOMS GET TO BE A MESS

IF YOU'RE FORTUNATE ENOUGH TO have a mudroom or a laundry room, you will quickly agree that, much like a kitchen, these areas take a beating. They are often crying out for storage space, because they're responsible for housing a range of items, like dirty clothes, backpacks, snow boots, and cleaning supplies. Wall hooks, labeled bins, and baskets are must-haves if you want to gain any amount of sanity and organization in these crazy spaces.

————

YOUR PLAN OF ACTION

Before you apply your organizational ESP and plan a new organizational system for your mudroom or laundry room, consider a few things that are unique to these areas of the home:

1) **Understand your needs.** The first thing you'll want to do is figure out what exactly you need from each space.

   For the Mudroom:
   - Is this where you enter and leave the house?
   - What type of items do you need to store there?
   - What is the simplest solution for me to get everyone on board: cubbies, hooks, maybe a bench?

   For the Laundry Room:
   - Do you need an area to hang clothes to dry?
   - How often do you do laundry?
   - Do you have accessible shelving?
   - Do you have ample storage?

2) **Create a drop zone:** Designate an area for outgoing mail, keys, and even reminders. You don't need a lot of wall space; usually a small area near the door will do the trick. You want to create a home for those important items that tend to get randomly dropped around the house.

3) **Simple always wins:** Avoid traditional closets that require people to stop and put things neatly away on hangers. It may sound crazy, but it adds an extra step in the process that most people like to skip. You have a better chance of your space staying organized if you keep the system simple by adding hooks for things like keys, purses, backpacks, and jackets.

4) **Create a cubby corner:** Whether you choose to do a locker-style set-up or a long bench with hooks and a shelf, make sure that everyone has a place for outerwear (like gloves, hats, and scarves). In the summer months, you can swap the cubbies for sunscreen, goggles, and baseball hats.

5) **Stack it:** If there is any chance for you to stack your washer and dryer, I say do it. The amount of space you gain is invaluable. If you want to gain even more space, install shelving or cabinets next to the stackable machines, and purchase the under-mount drawer that goes with the washer or dryer (I use it to store extra rags or towels).

6) **Install shelving or cabinets:** Depending on the size of your space, also consider adding open shelving or closed cabinetry anywhere you have unused wall space. Both provide great places to store supplies.

7) **Corral supplies:** Many people keep cleaning, household, or pet supplies in the laundry room. Use bins or baskets to keep bottles, jars, and containers neat and organized.

8) **Do a little at a time:** I recommend doing a little laundry each day rather than letting it build up until you have 10 loads to do on Sunday. Obviously, this

depends on how many people live in your home, but just like I recommend opening the mail each day, adding laundry to your list of daily chores is a more manageable way to stay ahead of the game.

———

Product Recommendations

- **Bins or baskets:** Good for storing things like rags, gloves, hats, scarves, or pet supplies.
  - Why I love them: Bins are one of the easiest and most inexpensive solutions to organizing a room. Throw a label on the front and you are good to go.
  - Where to get them: Online retailers like Amazon, Pottery Barn, Target, Wayfair, HomeGoods, The Container Store.
- **Sterilite Ultra bins:** Great for storing cleaning and laundry supplies.
  - Why I love them: Easy to wipe out, plus you can just grab your cleaning bin and go, rather than trying to hold a bunch of individual bottles.
  - Where to get them: Online retailers like Amazon, Target, The Container Store.
- **Hooks:** Best used in the mudroom or laundry room for hoodies, jackets, backpacks, purses, and dog leashes.
  - Why I love them: Hooks are simple and easy. They are by far one of my favorite grab-and-go

organizing solutions because they are so versatile and can add a stylish touch to any space.

o Where to get them: Online retailers like Amazon, Home Depot, Lowe's, Target, The Container Store.

* **Key holders & letter bins:** If you need a place to store keys and outgoing mail, there are some really cute options that don't take up a lot of space.

o Why I love them: Knowing exactly where my keys are every day saves me unnecessary stress and anxiety every morning. I don't have a ton of outgoing mail, since I do so much online, but it's still nice to have a place to stick a card that I want to send, instead of realizing three months later that it's sitting under a pile of papers on my desk.

o Where to get them: Online retailers like Wayfair, Ballard Designs, Pottery Barn, HomeGoods.

* **Mirrors:** If your mudroom or laundry room is where you enter and leave, it's nice to have a place to give a quick look to make sure you're good to go before heading out to face the world!

o Why I love them: It's just another little reason to give pause before we scurry about our hectic lives. We can all benefit from taking a moment to stop and just breathe before we face the world.

o Where to get them: Online retailers like Amazon, Target, Bed Bath & Beyond, HomeGoods.

CHAPTER 29

Craft Rooms & Wrapping Stations

WHY CRAFT ROOMS AND WRAPPING STATIONS GET TO BE A MESS

LET'S BE HONEST. MOST OF us do not have a beautifully decorated craft room like Martha Stewart. Even if we have the luxury of having a dedicated workspace, it very quickly can spiral out of control. Scraps of paper, embellishments, ribbons, and the like are all pesky gremlins that make it difficult to remain organized.

YOUR PLAN OF ACTION

Before you apply your organizational ESP and plan a new organizational system for your craft room or wrapping station, consider a few things that are unique to these areas of the home:

1) **Categorize.** The first step is to think about the various categories of items that you have and want to

organize. I bet it's more than you think. Below is a list of items to get you started:

- Wrapping paper rolls
- Tissue paper
- Gift bags
- Ribbon
- Gift tags
- Tape
- Glue sticks/glue gun
- Construction paper
- Stickers
- Fabric
- Glitter
- Crayons
- Markers
- Colored pencils
- Scissors
- Hole punch
- Rulers
- Sewing machine
- Sewing supplies
- Yarn
- Knitting or crochet needles

Once you have your list, you can begin to think about the best storage solutions for your space, budget, and habits. Ask yourself these necessary questions as you prepare to organize your space:

- Do I have room for a workstation?
- Do I like to stand and work or prefer to sit down?
- Do I want a desktop carousel for supplies, or would I prefer to have them in drawers?
- Do I prefer to see everything or have my items out of sight?

Product Recommendations

- **Desktop options:** You can find inexpensive desktop storage solutions that allow you organize your craft supplies and keep them where you need them.
  - Why I love them: There are a variety of options, from carousels that sit on your workspace to pull-out bins and drawers.
  - Where to find them: Online retailers like Amazon, Michaels, Jo-Ann Fabric and Craft Stores.
- **Wrapping paper storage containers:** I like to store long wrapping paper rolls in a tall hamper-like bin with wheels. The Container Store sells one that I own and recommend to clients quite a bit, and it actually can be found in the laundry section of the store—no joke.

- o Why I love them: Having the bin on wheels makes it easy to move from one spot to another (since I keep my wrapping paper in a closet, but tend to wrap in the kitchen).
- o Where to find them: Online retailers like Amazon, The Container Store.

* **Craft room furnishings:** Martha Stewart offers a line of craft room furniture and tabletop products online through Home Decorator Collection and Home Depot.
  - o Why I love them: If you are looking for pretty and functional, this definitely fits the bill. I am not going to lie, it's kind of a pain to put together, but if you have a lot of patience—or are willing to pay someone to do it for you—it's definitely worth a closer look.
  - o Where to find them: Online retailers like Home Decorator Collection or Home Depot.

* **Custom craft room makeovers:** If you are looking for a complete-room transformation, I like to use the Elfa storage system from The Container Store. They offer a variety of component options.
  - o Why I love them: Whether you need pegboards, drawers, or open shelving—they have it all. Best of all, they have a team of expert installers to get they system set up for you!
  - o Where to find them: The Container Store.

CHAPTER 30

Small Space Living

———

WHY SMALL SPACES GET TO BE A MESS

ANYONE WHO HAS EVER LIVED in an apartment, a shared a room, or an older home can relate to the struggles of small space living. Unlike the challenge of too much space with garages, basements, attics, and sheds, you find yourself storing your pots and pans in the oven and often struggle to find room for everything from memorabilia keepsakes to holiday decorations.

Another issue that often arises with small space living is that you may not have permission to add permanent structures, like built-ins or custom shelving, that could otherwise ease your storage woes.

Your small space may not have a guest room, basement, or attic, but I guarantee you can find room for what really matters. There are plenty of options out there; you may just have to get creative!

If you want to know a little secret, I LOVE the challenge of small space design and organizing. Not only does it force people to really think about what items they deem worthy of keeping in their homes, but it also allows you to get creative with how to make your space work for you. It can be challenging and fun to think outside the box and come up with nontraditional organizing solutions. If you need some small space help, give me a shout!

―――

Your Plan of Action

Before you apply your organizational ESP and plan a new organizational system for your small space, consider a few things that are unique to them:

1) **Understand your needs.** The first thing you want to determine is if your small space presents a volume issue (too much stuff), a layout issue (you don't have the right system to maximize the space), or a combination of both. If clutter is your issue, then the first thing to do is pare down. Once you've reduced the clutter from your space, the next step is to figure out what products would make your space more functional. For example, do you need more hanging space? Do you need more drawers? Would added shelving help solve your problem?

2) **Assess the space.** Look at your space and assess what you have to work with. Do you have high ceilings?

Deep closets? I have seen small homes and apartments that have tons of storage possibilities that are just not being maximized. If you get stuck and don't have the financial means to call in a professional, I recommend going on Pinterest or Houzz and searching for rooms with similar characteristics to see what creative solutions other people have used. Here are a few tips to get you started:

- **Look up:** The benefit of many small spaces is high ceilings. If you can, add shelving for infrequently used items. You may need a ladder to get up there, but who cares if the top shelves are used to store luggage or bins accessed once a year?

- **Divide and conquer:** Earlier, I mentioned a client who added a pressure wall to her NYC apartment and literally created a separate bedroom. If that's not in your budget, IKEA has some great bookshelves that can be used as room dividers. They not only help to create separate spaces, but add usable storage as well. I call that a win-win!

- **Impose double duty:** Invest in furniture that has built-in storage, such as a bed with drawers underneath, or an ottoman in which you can store blankets or board games. How about window seats for storing books or banquettes that can also hold linens? The options are endless.

———

Product Recommendations

- **Clear shoeboxes:** These are a must-have for small space living!
  - ○ Why I love them: They are not only great for storing shoes, but toys, cosmetics, tools, and other items.
  - ○ Where to get them: Online retailers like Amazon, Bed Bath & Beyond, Target, The Container Store.
- **Command Strips™:** These are a great option if you are not allowed to drill or hammer into a wall.
  - ○ Why I love them: Perfectly suited for hanging pet leashes, purses, sweatshirts, and other light-weight household items. Best of all, if you change your mind, you can take them down without any cleanup.
  - ○ Where to get them: Online, at your local hardware store, Staples, Target, most big-box stores.
- **Huggable velvet hangers:** They allow you to maximize your closet space and ensure your clothes sit at the same height.
  - ○ Why I love them: They are Inexpensive, space saving, and aesthetically pleasing.
  - ○ Where to get them: Online retailers like Amazon, Target, The Container Store, HomeGoods, HSN.
- **Hooks or wall-mount storage:** There are some great over-the-door hooks for apartments where you can't

drill. They are ideal for bathroom, bedroom or closet doors.

- o Why I love them: Wall-mount storage is another inexpensive way to add real estate to a small space.
- o Where to get them: Online retailers like Amazon, Bed Bath & Beyond, Target, HomeGoods, Home Depot, Lowe's, The Container Store.

"Getting organized is easy. Staying organized requires discipline."

—LAURIE PALAU

Moving Forward

———

I WISH I COULD TELL you that once you organize a space you are done forever; however, that is not quite the case. Like eating healthily or exercising, living clutter-free requires practice and discipline. There is no magic formula for how often you should revisit a space to stay on track. If you see things starting to derail, carve out time to get back on track before you lose control. Your ultimate goal for long-term success is figuring out a way to maintain a clutter-free lifestyle with minimal effort.

I realize that change is not always easy, especially when it comes to years of learned behavior, but the more you work at it, the easier it will be to make this your new way of living. I've been doing this for years, so of course it comes more naturally to me. With practice and discipline, you will find your groove too.

We covered a lot of ground. Now it's time for you to digest what you've read and start acting on it. The good news is that, unlike bodyweight—which is a lot harder to take off than to put on—you can reduce your clutter faster than you think. With a strategy and a usable system, you can put your mind to it.

Hopefully somewhere inside the pages of this book I've inspired you to face your clutter head on. I have no doubt that you can do this. If I can, you can! Although this isn't rocket science, it is a learned skill. The hardest part is figuring out how to get started, and I have mapped that out for you.

Living an organized life is something that should be incorporated into your world, not consume it. Instead of stressing over it, take it on as part of your regimen for health and well-being. Don't think that as soon as you finish this book, you have to purge the entire contents of your kitchen and start organizing. I suggest you start small and work within a realistic timeframe. Whether you have 15 minutes or an hour, remember that the goal is to incorporate these organizational strategies into your daily routine. If you set unattainable goals, you're setting yourself up for frustration. Your clutter didn't accumulate overnight, so don't expect it to disappear in the blink of an eye.

Your first job is to prioritize time in your day to do something small—even if it's sorting the mail, putting away the laundry, or getting in a routine of keeping dirty dishes out of the sink. The more you can slowly incorporate these daily strategies into your life, the easier it will be to maintain them.

Before I leave you, I want to remind you of some key takeaways:

1) **There are three main types of clutter:** Physical, emotional, and calendar. Identifying your dominant

source allows you to get to the root of your clutter issues and address them head on.

2) **There are five clutter pitfalls**: Procrastination, indecision, guilt, feeling overwhelmed, and time. Know where you get sucked in, and make a conscious effort to avoid it.

3) **Master your organizational ESP:** Empty, sort, and purge. It's a simple three-step method that can be used in any space by anyone.

4) **Remember the four piles:** Keep, donate, recycle, and relocate. If you do this, you will be sure to stay on task.

5) **Plan first, buy later.** Don't invest in products until you have developed a plan, prioritized your needs, and decluttered your space, so you know exactly what you need.

6) **Allocate space for memorabilia.** Keepsakes are important, but they need their own space. Be mindful of what you keep and why.

7) **Delegate.** Repeat after me: "I don't have to do everything myself!" As hard as this might be to believe, you can and should delegate things to your family. This

not only helps reduce calendar clutter, it empowers your family to take responsibility and own part of the process.

8) **Know your peak productivity time and that of those around you.** If you're a morning person, tackle tough tasks before the day gets away from you. The same holds true if you are a night owl. Don't waste time trying to embark on a project when you are not at the top of your game. It's only going to result in wasted time and frustration.

9) **Find a system that works for you.** We are all different; there is no one-size-fits-all method that works. It may take some trial and error, but you'll get there as long as you are consistent.

10) **Life is often hard. Life can get messy. That's okay.** If there's something in your life that is making you unhappy, work to fix it. If you need help, ask a friend. If that's not cutting it, ask an expert. Stop beating yourself up or comparing yourself to others. The truth of the matter is that we are all a bit of a Hot Mess, present company included, and that is what makes us real.

Resources

I'M NO DIFFERENT THAN YOU. I'm a busy person who doesn't have the time, money, or energy to waste trying to find what I need. To help you find resources that can help you get organized, I've broken this section is broken down into three areas: donations, products, and productivity. Hopefully you find these links useful!

For additional information and resources, visit my website: http://www.simplyborganized.com/

Social Links:

- Facebook: https://www.facebook.com/simplyBorganized/
- Twitter: https://twitter.com/smplyborganized
- Instagram: https://www.instagram.com/simplyborganized/
- LinkedIn: https://www.linkedin.com/in/simplyborganized/

- Pinterest: https://www.pinterest.com/smplyborganized/

Subscribe to my Podcast: This ORGANIZED Life

- Available on iTunes, Sound Cloud or Google Play

DONATIONS:

These are some of my favorite places for donations. Please visit each website and check your location for specific information on what items they accept. Many municipalities offer local pickup for bulk items, like appliances, once or twice a year. I recommend contacting your local government office or trash and recycling company to inquire whether this service is available.

My favorite places to donate stuff:

- Places of worship: Will often accept gently-used toys, books, and games.
- Greendrop: Offers both pick-up and drop off locations. Accepts clothing, shoes, household items, books and some electronics. https://www.gogreendrop.com/
- Habitat for Humanity: Accepts large furniture. https://www.habitat.org/
- Large appliances: Check local utility companies to see if they have a pickup program.
- Preschools: Will often accept gently-used toys, books, and games.
- The Salvation Army: Accepts cars, clothing, furniture, and household goods. https://satruck.org/
- Second Chance Toys: Accepts gently-used plastic toys. http://www.secondchancetoys.org/

- Local SPCAs and animal shelters: Will often accept unused pet food, supplies, old blankets, sheets, towels, and some pet toys.
- Vietnam Veterans of America: Accepts clothing, toys, small household items, bikes, books, electronics, tools, and sports equipment—and they pick up! http://pickupplease.org/

————

Products:

Although I can't tell you exactly what products you'll need without seeing your space, I can share links to some of the go-to places I mention in this book. There are plenty of other options out there; I'm simply letting you in on where I typically purchase products for myself and my clients, based on convenience, customer service, and cost.

My favorite places to shop for organizing products:

- Amazon: Check out the <u>storage and organization</u> section for everything from bins to hangers. https://www.amazon.com/
- Bed Bath & Beyond: My go-to place for kitchen drawer dividers. https://www.bedbathandbeyond.com/

- The Container Store: Specifically, I love their <u>Elfa</u> closet system and <u>Smart Store</u> system. https://www. containerstore.com/
- Home Depot: Great for storage racks, the <u>FastTrack</u> organizing system, and storage totes. http://www. homedepot.com/
- HomeGoods: Great finds at great prices! http://www. homegoods.com/
- IKEA: I love their <u>TROFAST</u> kids' storage system. http://www.ikea.com/
- The Land of Nod: They have an amazing selection of kids' furniture with built-in storage solutions. https:// www.landofnod.com/
- Organized Living: My favorite company for closet and garage systems. https://organizedliving.com/
- Pottery Barn: Specifically, I love their <u>Daily System</u> for home-office organization. https://www.potterybarn.com/
- See Jane Work: Stylish office supplies for women. http://www.seejanework.com/
- Staples: The one-stop shop for office supplies. https:// www.staples.com/
- Target: Find everything from Command Strips to <u>holiday storage</u>. https://www.target.com/
- Three by Three Seattle: Modern organizing supplies great for dorm rooms, offices, and command centers. https://threebythree.com/

- Wayfair: Great prices, wonderful customer service, and a great variety of indoor and outdoor products. https://www.wayfair.com/

———

PRODUCTIVITY APPS:

There are countless productivity apps available for both android and Apple devices. Just like organizing, everyone has an individual style and preference. I encourage you to explore the app store to try some out, but I'd be remiss if I didn't share my personal favorites. I have used each of the apps listed here on my phone.

My favorite productivity apps:

- All Recipes: Search for recipes, create an online recipe box, and even create shopping lists. http://allrecipes.com/
- Anylist: A great shopping-list app that allows you to group items by aisle, create favorites, and share with your family. https://www.anylistapp.com/
- ArtKive: A clutter-free way to store artwork. https://www.artkiveapp.com/
- CamCard: Upload business cards with the snap of your phone and instantly save to your address book. https://www.camcard.com/

- Dropbox: A free service that allows you to store your photos, docs, and videos anywhere and share them easily. https://www.dropbox.com/
- Evernote: An online notebook that syncs wirelessly between devices. The ultimate organizational app for easy searching and retrieval of notes, lists, and other important information. Share with your family or coworkers. https://evernote.com/
- Freedom: Blocks distracting apps and websites to help increase productivity. https://freedom.to/
- Google Drive: Allows users to store files in the cloud, synchronize files across devices, and share files. All you need is a free gmail account to get started. https://www.google.com/drive/
- Google Calendar: A free online calendar that you can customize, color-code, and share with family and co-workers. Quickly schedule meetings, set recurring events and get reminders about upcoming activities. https://calendar.google.com/
- Key Ring: Keeps all of your loyalty cards in one place (your phone!); no more searching your wallet for club cards. https://keyringapp.com/
- LastPass: Safely stores all of your passwords in one place. https://www.lastpass.com/
- Pepperplate: Manage recipes, create menus, plan meals, create shopping lists, and share with others. https://www.pepperplate.com/

- Pocket: The easiest way to save online articles in one place. I love it! https://getpocket.com/
- ScannerPro: Scans any papers, ranging from a receipt to multi-page documents. Instantly share, email, and upload. https://readdle.com/products/scannerpro
- Shutterfly: A safe and easy way to upload, share, and print your digital photos. Create albums for easy retrieval, so you can finally delete all those pictures from your phone and computer! https://www.shut-terfly.com/
- Unroll.me: The easiest way to declutter your inbox. Receive a list of all your subscription emails and unsub-scribe instantly to any you don't want. https://unroll.me/
- Wunderlist: My favorite list-making app. Use it for to-do lists, holiday lists, and everything in between, and customize, edit, and share. Syncs wirelessly between all your devices so you always have your lists with you. https://www.wunderlist.com/
- Yummly: Provides recipe recommendations person-alized to individual tastes and dietary restrictions, along with a digital recipe box, and sharing capabili-ties across social media. http://www.yummly.co/

ACKNOWLEDGMENTS

———

I WOULD BE REMISS WITHOUT taking time to recognize the countless people who have influenced parts of this book. First and foremost, my husband Joshua, and daughters, Zoe and Logan, who allow me to make them my human guinea pigs in the name of organization, and for fending for yourselves on several occasions so I could finish this book. To my friends, family and community, thank you all for your continued support of Simply B Organized through the years. Thanks to my organizing assistant, Erika Goodyear, for being my sounding board and keeping me in line when I start to derail. A special thank you to all of my clients who give me the opportunity to learn on a daily basis. To all the wonderful solutions providers who understand the need for simplicity and work to develop products and services to keep us organized. Last, but certainly not least, I thank my editors, Brandi Megan Granett and Marie Collins, for keeping my thoughts organized so this book could become a reality.

Made in the USA
San Bernardino, CA
24 May 2018